BABY BOOMER
GENERATION

THE
BABY BOOMER
GENERATION

A LIFETIME OF MEMORIES

PAUL FEENEY

To all the baby boomers we lost along the way

Front and back cover images courtesy of Mary Evans Picture Library: *front*: © Henry Grant; *back*: © John Gay/English Heritage

Originally published in hardback as 'From Ration Book to ebook: The Life and Times of the Post-War Baby Boomers', 2012 This paperback edition published in 2015

The History Press
The Mill, Brimscombe Port
Stroud, Gloucestershire, GL5 2QG
www.thehistorypress.co.uk

British Library Cataloguing in Publication Data.
A catalogue record for this book is available from the British Library.

ISBN 978 0 7509 6148 6

Typesetting and origination by The History Press
Printed in Great Britain

Contents

Acknowledgements

I would like to thank the following people and organisations for giving permission to reproduce photographs in this book: pages 4 (bottom), 5 (top), and 7 (top) Author/Remington Images. Pages 1 (top), 5 (bottom), 11 (top), and 16 (top and bottom) Getty Images. Page 2 (bottom) Gwen Lippingwell. Pages 3 (top) and 6 (bottom), Elizabeth Wallace. Page 4 (top) Picture Post/Getty Images. Page 6 (top) Gwen Lippingwell and Denise Baldwin. Page 8 (top) Josh Reynolds. Page 9 (bottom) John Gay/ English Heritage, NMR/Mary Evans. Page 10 (top left) Mary Evans Picture Library/Bill Coward. Page 13 (bottom) Mary Evans/The Watts Collection. Page 14 (top) *Illustrated London News*/Mary Evans. All other pictures and illustrations are from the author's collection. Every reasonable care has been taken to avoid any copyright infringements, but should any valid issue arise then I will look to correct it in subsequent editions.

Preface

It would take a lifetime's work and a volume of books to explain the complete history of life in Britain post-1945. This book is intended to provide a condensed insight into the life and times of those who were born in the years immediately following the Second World War when there was a sharp increase in the birth rate, known as the baby boom. There was another baby boom in the early 1960s and because of that the period from 1946 to 1964 is often referred to as the baby boom period. However, the term 'post-war baby boomer' is used to describe the generation born between 1946 and 1952. This book covers the period from 1945 to 2012 and I hope it will act as a valuable lesson in British social history for young and old alike. More importantly, I trust it will serve to jog memories of times gone by for anyone who was around in the days before television took control of our lives and the nation became obsessed with modern-day consumerism. Above all, this trip back in time will touch each and every member of the post-war baby-boomer generation and remind them of their own journey through life, from as far back as their childhood in the austere Britain of the 1940s and 1950s, through to the smart technological age we live in today. The country and our whole way of life have changed beyond recognition and there is no going back, but we need to remember the past and learn from it, and some of us just need to wallow in the joys of nostalgia from time to time.

Paul Feeney

one

1940s

Victory and the Post-War Baby Boom

A t 7.40 p.m. on Monday 7 May 1945, BBC Radio reported
that Germany had surrendered to the Allies and the war
in Europe was over. It was declared that Tuesday 8 May would
be an official day of celebration and a public holiday, which
would be called Victory in Europe (VE) Day. The prime minister,
Winston Churchill, was to make an official announcement the
following afternoon. A whole week had gone by since news had
reached us that Hitler had shot himself in the mouth and the
British people were growing increasingly frustrated because, as
yet, there had been no official broadcast from 10 Downing Street,
and now Churchill was going to make everyone wait another
day. There were rumours that German delegates had visited

Field Marshal Montgomery's headquarters in Lüneburg Heath in northern Germany to surrender their armies to the Western Allies, but we knew nothing for certain. There was a shroud of secrecy over events and we didn't know what was delaying the official announcement. The British people were not told at the time, but there were very good reasons why the war had dragged on for those extra few days. One reason was that the Allies were insistent they would only accept an unconditional surrender from Germany and nothing less. Then there was the problem with the German troops who had chosen to continue fighting the Russian Red Army on the Eastern Front rather than being captured by them, because they feared that the Russians might seek cruel retribution for the atrocities committed against their people during the German invasion of Russia. The final delaying factor was that the Allies had bowed to Russia's insistence that the unconditional surrender be kept secret until Wednesday 9 May, but this agreement was scuppered by the Germans when they broke the news to their own people on German radio at 2.27 p.m. on Monday 7 May, and word of it soon spread around the world. Hence, everyone knew the war in Europe was over but the British public needed to hear it first-hand from the prime minister himself.

Meanwhile, throughout Britain, shop windows had been decked-out with tri-coloured rosettes and banners in anticipation of Churchill's imminent declaration of peace in Europe. At least the public now knew that they only had to wait one more day to hear Churchill's official broadcast. The interim news report of Germany's surrender was enough to trigger an immediate release of the tension that had been building up for several days. It was a big relief to everyone; it was as if people suddenly felt able to breathe again and the feeling of liberation produced a spontaneous outpouring of emotion. The public could not contain their overwhelming feeling of joy and they made it clear that they had no intention of waiting until the next day to begin celebrating their victory in Europe. All at once, a sea of red, white and blue began to spread across the nation; bunting was hung in criss-cross patterns along the streets and Union Jacks were draped from upstairs' windows and lampposts. Although the mood in the country was a mixture of jubilation and sombre reflection, there was an irresistible desire for everyone to celebrate. The public outburst of pent-up emotion was not confined to a number of brash exhibitionists playing to an audience of onlookers; the news was so good that it inspired thousands of ordinary men and women, who would not usually say boo to a goose, to temporarily shed their inhibitions and dance in the street alongside complete strangers.

In London, where the biggest celebrations took place, the street scenes portrayed an atmosphere of unbridled happiness, which created a mood of genuine friendliness among people from all walks of life. Thousands of revellers besieged the areas around Piccadilly Circus and Trafalgar Square and the noisy festivities continued on throughout the evening. As night fell it became quite dark because there were no streetlights due to the blackout rules, but this did not deter the revellers. Adopting their typical wartime 'make do' attitude, the crowds used newspapers to build small bonfires on the pavements to supplement beams of light emanating from night buses, which were slowly weaving their way through the hordes of high-spirited people filling the main roads. Even the overnight storm did not dampen the ever-increasing euphoria generating from the growing crowds. The police estimated that by midnight there were 50,000 people packed into Piccadilly Circus and celebrations were continuing to gather pace throughout London, and in every other town and city around the country. That evening, for the first time since the war began, the BBC was allowed to broadcast the weather forecast and it promised good weather ahead.

The merriment carried on overnight and Tuesday 8 May, VE Day, turned out to be a glorious summer's day. People wore their Sunday best and women added to the cheerfulness of the day by sporting brightly coloured summer dresses. Newspaper headlines shouted 'Germany Surrenders'. In London, there was hardly a cloud in the sky: perfect weather for the thousands of people who had crammed themselves into Trafalgar Square, Parliament Square and other public areas around central London to hear the King's speech, which was to be relayed on specially erected loudspeakers. The country was very loyal to King George VI and the people undoubtedly shared the sentiment shown in his heart-rending 'Thanksgiving' speech that day, but it was the words of Prime Minister Winston Churchill that they were most eager to hear. Their patience was eventually rewarded at 3.00 p.m. that day when Churchill made his famous 'End of War in Europe' speech to the nation, broadcast live from the Cabinet Room at 10 Downing Street. In it, he announced that Germany had signed the act of unconditional surrender at 2.41 a.m. the previous day at the Supreme Headquarters Allied Expeditionary Force in Rheims, France. Churchill confirmed that the ceasefire was already in place and that hostilities would end officially at one minute past midnight that night. The assembled crowds cheered loudly and waved their flags even more vigorously when they heard Churchill say the words 'God bless you all. This is your victory!' Hearing this touching phrase sparked renewed outbursts of loud cheering and enthusiastic flag-waving from the crowds of proud and happy people who had congregated in open spaces in every town and city across the length and breadth of the country. Church bells rang out throughout the land to mark the momentous occasion.

In London, the tightly packed areas around Whitehall echoed with the sounds of rapturous shouts of approval, which rebounded off the walls of government buildings and tall office blocks. On hearing Churchill's words, 'This is your victory!' the crowd roared back, 'No, it's yours!' in acknowledgement of Churchill being the hero of the day. Everybody starting kissing one another and some formed themselves into lines to have a knees-up and sing popular pub songs like 'Knees Up Mother Brown' and 'The Lambeth Walk'. All of a sudden, from out of nowhere, musicians began to arrive on the scene, playing all kinds of musical instruments, from accordions to barrel organs. Upright pianos were dragged out of local pubs into the street and groups of British and Allied servicemen and women, arm in arm with civilians, gathered around to sing their favourite wartime songs. They belted out their own renditions of 'It's a Long Way to Tipperary' and 'Roll Out The Barrel', many sounded like a cats' chorus but nobody cared. With rolled-up trousers and hitched-up skirts, men and women frolicked in the fountains of Trafalgar Square. The lower ledges of Nelson's Column were full to overflowing with excited onlookers while others sat astride each of the four monumental bronze lions, flag-waving and cheering. Fathers carried their young children shoulder high to protect them from the crushing crowds. All over the country, in the local backstreets there were thousands of children's street parties in full swing, with youngsters laughing and grinning in between mouthfuls of cake and jelly: party food they had only ever before dreamed of. There was a great show of pride and patriotism throughout the nation. Everybody wore something in colours of red, white and blue; even small children and babies had tri-colour ribbons in their hair and pet dogs were tagged with patriotic rosettes and decorative bows. Back in London, as evening fell, more and more people converged on the area around Trafalgar Square to see London's great monuments illuminated, floodlit specially for the occasion. There were firework displays all around the capital and effigies of Hitler were burned on bonfires. Then, after six long years of blackout, the streetlights came on. This was another welcome sight to highlight the fact that the war in Europe really was over. Some people found the party atmosphere too manic and the crushing crowds too hard to bear. And so, having set off early to travel into the capital from the outer suburbs of London and the Home Counties, they went home. When they got there, some joined in with local celebrations while others allied themselves to the many who had chosen to spend their time at home in quiet reflection. All around the country, people marked the day in many different ways, but everybody went to bed that night knowing that they could at last sleep in peace. There would be no air-raid sirens and no bombs to fear, but they would never forget what had gone before.

During the war, few British towns or cities escaped the bombardments from enemy aircraft, with Bootle, Hull, Birmingham and Coventry being among those that suffered the most. But, from the start of the Blitz in September 1940 and throughout the war, it was London that took the brunt of the incessant German bombing raids and suffered the most destruction and the highest number of casualties. Now, at long last, people would no longer need to fear the terrifying buzzing sound of approaching German V-1 flying bombs or Doodlebugs, as they were commonly known, and the newer and even more terrifying V-2 rockets, which travelled faster than the speed of sound and gave no warning before impact. Nevertheless, residents in urban areas of the country were haunted by recollections of the sheer terror they had experienced during the war. The enormous amount of destruction and the indiscriminate killings these missiles inflicted on innocent civilians were all too fresh in their memories. Those who were fortunate enough to have escaped any bodily damage still carried the mental scars of war: vivid memories of enemy attacks and the loved ones they had lost, the sound of victims' cries for help coming from beneath the rubble of bombed and collapsed houses, and the horrible smell of burning buildings and powdered brick dust that regularly filled the air. It had only been six weeks since the very last German V-2 missiles had fallen on London, on 27 March 1945, one having made a direct hit on Hughes Mansions in the Stepney area of London, killing 134 residents and leaving 49 seriously injured. On that same day, the final V-2 had landed in Orpington, Kent, killing housewife Mrs Ivy Millichamp, who was the last civilian to die as a result of enemy action over Britain during the Second World War. The horrors and torment of war were indelibly stamped upon everyone's mind and nerves remained very raw. Despite this, there were few who could suppress the happiness they now felt in the knowledge that those six long years of wartime destruction and misery were now at an end. At last, Nazism had been defeated.

Meanwhile, the war against Japan in Asia and the Pacific continued unabated, but that war was also expected to end soon. It did so shortly after the USA dropped two atomic bombs, one on Hiroshima and the other on Nagasaki. Just three months after the Allied victory over Germany in Europe, the Japanese emperor, Hirohito, made a radio broadcast announcing Japan's unconditional surrender. The Allies declared the historic day of Wednesday 15 August 1945 to be Victory over Japan (VJ) Day and it was to be marked by a two-day holiday in the UK, the USA and Australia. Once again the people took to the streets and the scenes of jubilation were repeated. For the British people, this was the ultimate celebration because it marked the end of the horrible world war. No more British servicemen and women need die in battle and loved ones could start to come home. The biggest conflict in history, the Second World War, formally ended on 2 September 1945, several days after the VJ Day celebrations, when the Japanese finally signed the surrender document on board the American battleship, USS *Missouri*, in Tokyo Bay.

Amidst the excitement of Britain's victory celebrations, there were many people who had to face up to crucial and sometimes upsetting changes that the war had caused in their personal lives. There was a coming together of war-torn families, friends and sweethearts, and some of these reunions were not at all easy. Many child evacuees returned home as strangers to their parents, having spent their formative childhood years living with foster parents miles from home. Some never managed to adjust to their change in circumstances, rejecting their real parents and wanting to go back to their foster parents. After all, imagine a 12-year-old child returning to a war-torn inner-city home after having lived in a quiet country village as part of a loving adoptive family since the age of 6. It was hard for all concerned; the homecoming children often spoke with unfamiliar regional accents they had picked up from local people in the area they had been evacuated to, and their real home life was very different from what they had been used to when living in the country. For some, having spent such a long time apart, even their brothers and sisters were now strangers to them. Not all siblings had been evacuated during the war, however, many children stayed at home or returned home within weeks of being evacuated and so their family bond was not broken, unlike those who had spent years away from home. It was a very difficult and sad situation; there were parents who felt guilty for having sent their children away to the country and some children carried the mental scars of evacuation with them for the rest of their lives.

Then there were the problems of battle-weary servicemen returning home from war. Many had been changed physically or mentally, or both, by the effects and the long duration of the war. Young people in particular struggled to come to terms with each other's new behaviour as time spent apart sometimes turned a one-time lover into a stranger. The young teenage boys who went off to war six years before were returning home as full-grown men, often shell-shocked and traumatised by the horrifying things they had witnessed. They longed to see their sweethearts who in younger days had sworn their undying love, but sadly, some were not waiting at home with open arms as they were expected to be. They too had experienced the strains of war, having been left at home to suffer the austere times and to witness all the wartime distress while, at the same time, living in an environment in which there was a distinct shortage of young men. A lot of these young women had found themselves living and working in strange surroundings, doing jobs they would never have dreamed of doing and having to live temporarily in places that were unfamiliar to them. To help the war effort, the majority of eligible women had worked in various skilled and labouring occupations that would have normally been done by men, from working in dangerous munitions factories to labouring for long hours in the fields as Land Girls in the Women's Land Army. Most of the other eligible women either joined or were conscripted into one of the many women's auxiliary services, like the ATS (Auxiliary Territorial Service), the Wrens (Women's Royal Naval Service), the WAAFs (Women's Auxiliary Air Force), the WTS (Women's Transport Service) and the WVS (Women's Voluntary Service). Some even did service overseas, particularly those special women who undertook highly dangerous roles in the SOE (Special Operations Executive). Women also served alongside men in the fire, police, air transport and air raid and anti-aircraft services. All in all, about 90% of women took an active part in the British war effort. This was one of the hidden consequences of the war, suffered by many families; everyone and everything had changed to some extent and people had to get to know one another again.

Each and every family knew of some unfortunate person who had been killed during the conflict or had his or her home destroyed, and there was still a lot of grieving to be done. The young had been forced to grow up quickly and to do without many of the frivolities usually enjoyed as part of one's youth. Everyone sacrificed a lot over a long period of time to help secure our country's freedom and to create a safer world for future generations to live in. These young men and women now yearned for the dawning of a new Britain – one that would be filled with opportunities to improve their standard of living and provide a better future for all – and they had helped to lay new foundations on which their children could grow up and prosper without the dreadful burden of war hanging over them. Parents could now happily leave their new-born babies in prams outside their street doors to enjoy the fresh air without fear of enemy bombing raids and the resulting pollution. People were at last able to plan for the future in the knowledge that employment prospects were good, housing and social services were destined to improve, and the country was a safe place in which to live and bring up children.

There were lots and lots of new-born babies in the mid- to late forties. Most were either planned or allowed to happen but there were also many surprise and unwanted pregnancies. The country was in a triumphant mood and young adults had lots of pent-up tension to release at a time when methods of birth control were limited and unreliable. It was inevitable that there would be unwanted pregnancies and that some young couples, and principally young women, would have to suffer the consequences for their moment of unbridled passion. Sadly, countless numbers of young unmarried girls were left holding the baby, the fathers having either disappeared altogether or ducked out of their parenting responsibilities. In those days, there was a real stigma attached to an unmarried woman giving birth to a baby. Whether the father was on the scene or not, the child was still considered to be illegitimate and would be referred to as a bastard. It was regarded as shameful to have a child outside of marriage and it brought scandal on the whole family. As a consequence, pregnant young girls were often spirited away to 'unmarried mothers' homes where they would be pressured into giving up their new-born baby for adoption. This practice continued on into the fifties.

All in all, there was a huge increase in births after the war, peaking in 1947 when the annual birth rate rose to just short of a million. The increase went some way to repopulating the nation, which had been reduced by 450,000 during the war. By the end of 1947 the UK population was 49.4 million, rising to 50.2 million by 1952. All those born from 1946 to 1952 were to make up what would become known as the first wave of the post-war baby-boomer generation. More baby boom periods would follow in the late-1950s and through to the mid-1960s, but the period immediately following the war is the time that most people associate with the birth of the baby boomers. It was these babies who were to become the innocent children of the fifties and the pioneering teenagers of the 1960s. Born to parents who had only known hardship and suffering for most of their lives, it was hoped that these baby boomers would grow up in a safer world that would be full of opportunity.

The nation was eager to get started on rebuilding the country's damaged and worn-out cities and to help create the new dawn that had been promised for us all. However, within two months of Churchill being hailed as the hero of the hour, the British public turfed him out of office. In the July 1945 general election, the people of the United Kingdom decided that the man who had led Britain so well in war was not the man to lead the nation in peace, and instead they elected a new Labour Government into office. Clement Attlee became the new prime minister with a mandate to change the face of Britain, to maintain full employment and greatly enlarge our system of social services. Our parents and grandparents had now started the ball rolling. Their aim was to create a better future for us baby boomers. They didn't know where it would lead but they wanted their children to have greater opportunities and to strive for more than they could have ever hoped for.

Britain in the 1940s allowed few opportunities for young people to better themselves and so their ambitions were usually simple ones: to get a job and put food on the table, the same as it had been for generations. Some managed to break out of the mould but those with limited education would more often than not become industrial workers doing some sort of manual work, which would usually mean performing the same tasks on just one machine for the rest of their working lives. There was plenty of work available but where you lived often determined the type of work you did. If you grew up in a mining village then from an early age you were destined to go down the mines. A grammar school education was a route to a profession, but for most working-class people the idea of developing a career was not something they even thought about. When kids left school at the age of 14 or 15 their only concern was to get a job and to keep it; it was both a matter of pride and necessity to be in regular work. Family members of working age were expected to contribute a sizable proportion of their take-home pay towards housekeeping costs. Many youngsters gave their pay packet to their mum at the end of each week and she would give them back a small amount of money each day to pay for their travel and get them through the day; the rest would go towards the housekeeping. Even highly motivated young people found it very hard to carve out a worthwhile career. British employers were not particularly efficient in the way they ran their businesses. It was all very traditional, following a well-trodden path handed down from the generations before. Managers didn't go to business school but instead learned their skills through their own boss. This was a hopeless situation because most business leaders were ex-public schoolboys who had no management skills themselves. Nepotism was rife in business and there was a huge gap between management and workers. Men ran industry and they employed men for any skilled and managerial jobs, while women worked on assembly lines, did the typing, ran errands and made the tea. The poor management skills and the short-sightedness of untrained people at the top set the tone for the way British industry was run and helps explained why, as a manufacturing nation, we were achieving such poor productivity. Our manufacturing industry was providing lots of jobs and producing all the right things, but we could not efficiently produce enough. It was difficult for business bosses to see where they were going wrong; many had blinkers on and were living in the past. At the same time, it was difficult for fresh blood to break through the glass ceiling put in place by the 'old boys' brigade and any new ideas put forward to change business practices were frowned upon.

It was a hard task for anyone from a working-class background to become a senior manager, and it was almost impossible for women. Many employers shied away from employing anyone who showed signs of having ambition. They tended to look no further than covering an immediate requirement for someone to perform a single task, like an office worker who could add up a row of figures or a girl who could type a letter. A supervisor would be used to keep an eye on workers and make sure they didn't skive off or pinch anything, rather than devise ways to improve efficiency. A factory worker with initiative was seen as a hindrance rather than an asset; the boss just wanted someone who could operate a lever 1000 times a day. There were also no rules about equality in the workplace. It was quite legal for employers to specify exactly what type of person they were looking for when placing job adverts, including age, gender, colour, religion, height, weight or whatever. And, once employed, there was nothing to protect employees from bad employers other than the limited protection offered by the trade unions, which usually meant the threat of strike action. There were no health and safety rules and no legal requirement for employers to treat workers with respect or to pay them a reasonable wage. Membership of trade unions was an established part of working life in Britain and as our businesses struggled to compete in the post-war world, the trade unions became more aggressive and powerful. There was an invisible barrier between workers and management and there were no common objectives. Industrial workers felt they were hard done-by, often working in dangerous and generally bad conditions, poorly paid and with no job security.

In the 1940s city, the early morning street scene was of men and women trudging to work with smoke drifting from dog-ends hidden beneath hundreds of anonymous flat caps and scarves. Others on bicycles expertly weaved their way through the throng, many gripping roll-ups between their teeth and puffing away as they went. The rush to work was not spurred on by enthusiasm but the need to clock in on time. Work was a necessary chore and for most there was no expectation of job satisfaction at the end of each day and nothing better to look forward to at work the next day. Many had to endure awful working conditions; miners suffered dangerous, dark, dirty and cramp conditions underground, while factory workers risked life and limb on each shift by manually operating unguarded machines for long hours in overcrowded, noisy and dirty factories. A cushy office job wasn't the perfect alternative, as office workers were closely supervised and often worked in cramped and untidy conditions, forced to breathe air that was usually filled with cigarette smoke. Accidents were an everyday occurrence in the 1940s workplace, especially for the industrial workers.

The homes that many of us early baby boomers were born into in the late 1940s were very simple in comparison to today. Apart from the noticeable absence of any labour-saving machines and electronic devices, there were only a small number of people with television sets; only about 400 wealthy households in and around London had one. At the time, the service from the Alexandra Palace transmitter in North London only covered a radius of 40 to 100 miles on a good day, and even the wealthy families who had bought a television when transmissions first began in 1936 had not been able to switch them on since war broke out in 1939 because the transmitter was shut down and the BBC's television service only resumed in 1946. The service was extended to cover the Midlands in 1949 but the rest of the country had to wait a few more years. It didn't really matter because televisions were a real luxury item: too expensive for most wage earners. There was also a newly introduced television licence fee to pay. The television may be today's main instrument of home entertainment but it was not part of home life in the late 1940s Britain. As our mothers sat cradling us new-born babies in their arms, their only distraction was the soothing sounds coming from a huge valve wireless set on top of the sideboard. Mum's fireside cuddle and the deep comforting tones of radio were all that were needed to send us off to the Land of Nod.

Houses were by no means cosy, but in between fighting off drafts from every corner of the house our parents did their best to make our early years as comfortable as possible. Having practiced a 'make do and mend' way of life for the past six years, they now wanted more for themselves and their children. The restrictive 1940s lifestyle had been forced on them at a very young age and they missed out on so much of their youth. Many of them were still at school when war broke out in 1939 and they were never able to properly enjoy their teenage years. However, the war was now over and they were still young, many in their late teens and early twenties and with their whole lives ahead of them. Times were still hard and rationing was on going but things could only get better. Everybody knew that the country was up to its neck in debt to America and almost bankrupt, so they had no real idea what the future held for them. It was difficult to understand how we were going to get out of debt while at the same time rebuild the country. There were a lot of big hurdles to overcome and it seemed a mountain of a task that would take years to achieve. Although grateful for what they had, they wanted to see improvements in their overall standard of living and as soon as possible. The government wasn't going to give away any hand-outs and the only option was for them to work hard, even if they hated the job they did. Anyway, the idea that anybody could be privileged enough to live the dream – a job they loved doing in a workplace they looked forward to going to each day and a comfortable home to return to each night – was just a fairy-tale to the post-war working classes, but they knew there had to be a better way of life ahead.

Baby boomers who were born before midnight on 4 July 1948, when the National Health Service (NHS) first came into operation, were more of a worry to their young parents than those born after. Before the start of the National Health Service, there was no free health care. Apart from the elderly and mentally ill who were looked after by local authority-run hospitals, only people with jobs were entitled to free medical treatment, which was made possible under a workers' health insurance scheme, but the free treatment often didn't cover other members of the family, even their children. It wasn't all plain sailing for the workers who were covered under the scheme; they had to pay upfront and claim it back afterwards. Wealthy people could afford to pay for the best treatment or, alternatively, they could choose to take out expensive insurance to protect their families. Everyone else had to save up enough money before they could get treatment, otherwise they had to rely on charities or do what most people did – resort to home remedies, many of which were questionable and sometimes dangerous. There were charity doctors but they usually only gave their services free to the poorest patients; others had to find the money or do without. Those with poor eyesight could buy their spectacles at Woolworth for sixpence. For the pre-NHS baby boomers, surviving the first year of life was a feat in itself, with one in twenty babies dying before their first birthday. And, if the freezing cold houses of wintertime didn't kill you, there were always the infectious killer diseases like pneumonia, meningitis, tuberculosis, diphtheria and polio. It must have felt like Christmas when the National Health Service finally became operational. It was a great relief to everyone, particularly to women with young children.

On that first morning there were long queues of people waiting for doctors' surgeries to open. People with long-term medical problems could at last seek help and the nations' young mothers could now better protect their children's health. Our health! – the post-war baby boomers: the first generation to enjoy the benefits of the National Health Service.

two

Childhood Austerity and Innocence

Having endured years of hardship and witnessed the terrible atrocities of war, our parents and grandparents were at last enjoying the freedom and peace they fought so long and hard for. The victory came at an enormous personal cost to British families, with 450,900 loved ones killed during the hostilities, including 60,595 civilians who lost their lives in enemy air raids and rocket attacks, with countless numbers of survivors left physically and mentally scared. By the end of the 1940s, however, the euphoria felt by the victorious British people when the war ended in 1946 had faded into distant memory. Individual families struggled to put their lives back together, while at the same time the whole nation was feeling the pinch as the country faced up to the huge financial costs of the conflict. The war had left Britain up to the hilt in debt to the USA and Canada. The country was almost bankrupt and it was going to take us decades to pay off the combined loans of US$5.52 billion, an amount that would have the same buying power as US$66 billion in 2011 (the final payment on these loans was made in December 2006). We were at peace but most of us were destined to continue living austere lives for the foreseeable future. Although life had not been as easy since the war ended as people had expected, you could still sense that folk had a great pride and loyalty to their country and they seemed to share a common purpose in life. The post-war feeling of solidarity was still very evident around the country and there was a proper sense of friendliness and trust among the people in local communities. Families tended to stay together and live close to one other, and everyone knew their neighbours and had a sense of belonging. There was a great feeling of trust between neighbours and it was common practice for people to leave their doors unlocked when they were in, and to hang a key behind the letterbox when they went out. There were lots of families with small children and so there were plenty of young mothers around to keep an eye out for strangers and for anyone who might be up to no good; it was a sort of unofficial neighbourhood watch. There were plenty of scallywags around but there were far fewer burglaries and robberies than there are today. With the unofficial band of Neighbourhood Watch and a plentiful supply of Bobbies out pounding their beats, there was a good chance of would-be burglars getting caught and this deterred many thieves. Most people in working-class neighbourhoods had little worth stealing anyway. The vast majority of people had a very strong work ethic with little expectation of getting something for nothing. There were plenty of jobs around and so there was less of an excuse for anyone to steal things. The need to fund a drug addiction was very rare in those days and there was no peer pressure for people to wear fashionable clothes or to have all the latest gadgets and other flashy possessions. Burglars and thieves were not as brazen as they are today; they were much more fearful of being seen in case they were recognised and caught. The punishments were much tougher then, even for petty crimes, and there was the feeling of disgrace at being branded a thief because a tremendous cloud of shame would descend over the whole family of anyone who got into trouble with the police.

Family ties were considered to be very important and people commonly held what would now be considered old-fashioned, down-to-earth values at time when the country as a whole had a good moral structure. It was very unusual to know someone with a criminal record. A high street bank was more likely to get robbed than any working-class family home.

Our parents had become used to doing without many of the things that we now regard as essentials. During the war, they had learned how to use things sparingly by efficiently managing the government's endless list of rationed goods, including meat, butter, lard, margarine, sugar, tea, coffee, soap, clothing, petrol and sweets. The end of war, however, had not signalled the end of rationing. In fact, the rules governing rationing were made even stricter in the aftermath of war than they had been during the war. Bread and potatoes had not previously been rationed in the UK but the Ministry of Food put bread and flour on ration from 21 July 1946 to 25 July 1948, and potatoes were put on ration in the autumn of 1947 through until 30 April 1948. Other goods remained on ration until well into the 1950s, with tea coming off the list in 1952, sugar and eggs in 1953 and finally cheese and meats in 1954 when all rationing ended. Our parents had experienced life before rationing first began in 1940 and they had found it hard to get used to living within the strictly enforced limits. The harsh rationing system meant they had to get by on much smaller quantities of the everyday essentials, which they had been used to having in unlimited quantities before the war began. They were forced to adapt their whole way of life to conform to the rationing system and learn to get by with much less of everything; they certainly felt deprived, and they were. By 1954, having already suffered fourteen years of official rationing, they were resigned to the fact that it would be a few more years before they would see a return to the good times, but it was all very different for us children because we had been born into a world of rationing and we didn't feel deprived because we had never known anything different. Each day, our mothers struggled with the task of how to best utilise the rationed items to satisfy the needs of the whole family and we children came to think of this as being a normal part of housekeeping. In the worst of times, some children will have been undernourished but the majority of us usually had enough to eat and didn't find it hard to live within the restraints of rationing; we didn't even think about it. We thought it was normal for our mums to carry ration books with them whenever they went out shopping and as far as we knew it had always been that way. We were used to running errands armed with the appropriate ration book and we considered this to be normal. In the same way, we thought that kids had always spent their childhoods playing on bomb sites and exploring derelict buildings. We didn't regard our upbringing as being in any way unusual and most of us didn't really feel deprived of anything. After all, we never shared our mothers' concerns over how to make a small scrag-end of mutton into a healthy family meal. Mind you, we had no real choice in what we ate; we just ate what was put in front of us. There was no such thing as a fussy eater and phrases like, 'I don't like this,' and 'I'm not eating that,' were never used. We had never known what it was like to have a choice. To us it was just food that we needed to eat regularly for nourishment and energy. If we were hungry between meals, we knew that the quickest way to a full belly was a doorstep of bread. As young children, we were aware that sweets were not freely available to buy and so we never got into the habit of nagging our mums to buy them when we were out at the shops. We grew up believing that chocolate and other sweets were luxuries, something you only had occasionally as a special treat. Mind you, we did go a bit mad when sweet rationing was lifted on 5 February 1953. On that day, we all raided our piggy banks and headed off to the local sweetshops. It was a very special day; the shopkeepers were besieged with hordes of neighbourhood kids, all desperate to buy one or two treats from the huge selection of unrationed sweets on display. Penny chews, boiled sweets, nougat and liquorice sticks were all very popular but, surprisingly, it was toffee apples that were the biggest sellers of the day. A firm in South London gave away 800 free lollipops to local kids, while other manufacturing companies handed out free sweets to anyone who turned up at their factory gates. It was all very exciting: a one-off experience that was unlikely to ever happen again. We had an extra special spring in our step that day; it was certainly a day to remember. Knowing that sweets were now available to buy in unlimited quantities didn't immediately turn us into chocoholics. Having spent our early years doing without sweets, we had no addiction to them and most of us continued to regard them as treats, preferring to buy a comic than a packet of Spangles. Strangely enough, although sweets were now de-rationed, we had to wait another few months before sugar was taken off rationing in September 1953.

The post-war baby-boomer generation was still at pre-school age when the clocks crept past midnight to herald the arrival of the first New Year of the 1950s. The population of the United Kingdom had just passed the 50 million mark and three-quarters of all families lived in rented accommodation. A quarter of British homes had no electricity and Britain still had an empire, albeit a diminishing one. Everyone, including children, were compelled to carry wartime identity cards wherever they went and this requirement continued right up until 1952, seven years after the war had ended. Trams were still in use on our city streets and they carried on running for another two years. The vast majority of our parents were married before we were born, with only 3% of us born outside of marriage. Abortion and homosexual acts were illegal and capital punishment still existed. The British way of life was very different back then; there were no shopping centres, multiplex cinemas and out of town retail parks. Self-service stores and supermarkets had been popular in America since the 1930s but it took the British a long time to catch up. A handful of self-service shops opened here during the 1940s and J. Sainsbury opened their first one in Croydon in 1950, but other food chains were slow to follow Sainsbury's lead; by the end of the decade self-service stores were still few and far between.

Shopping in individual specialist shops was still the norm here. With many families living hand-to-mouth and few homes having refrigerators, there was an essential need for daily shopping and the corner shop was at the centre of the local community. They usually sold everything from newspapers to sliced ham, but unlike today, most of them didn't open in the evening and they shut for a half-day during the week, with some shutting all day on Mondays. Our mothers did their weekly shopping in the local high street, nipping in and out of many different shops, including the butcher's, baker's and greengrocer's. There was also a busy local pub on nearly every street corner of the land where noisy singsongs could be heard bellowing out on a Saturday night.

For most of the 1950s, the wireless (radio) was our main source of entertainment in the home. At the turn of the century, two out of three people in Britain had never seen a television programme let alone owned a television set. Television ownership only started to take off in 1953, prompted by the public's desire to see the coronation of Queen Elizabeth II, which was planned to be broadcast live on BBC television in June that year. There was another surge in sales of television sets when Independent television (ITV) first began broadcasting commercially funded television programmes to the London region in September 1955, and sales continued to increase each year as ITV gradually rolled out its regional broadcasting coverage. By the end of the 1950s, three-quarters of the population had access to a television set.

Throughout the 1950s, cinema was our main source of entertainment outside of the home. With only limited access to television programmes, it was the only way we could see what was going on outside of our own little cocoons. It also provided us with the means to escape from our usual humdrum existence: for a few hours we could enter a world of pure fantasy. There were so many wonderful British and American films for us to enjoy and even us kids liked to watch the Pathé newsreel with its dramatic voice-over narrations. We were so captivated by these films that three-quarters of us went to the cinema at least once a week and we would happily queue for up to an hour outside in the rain for the one-and-nine-penny seats, and then, at the end of the main film, everyone would stand while the National Anthem was played. As time went by we noticed that cinemas were beginning to interrupt the films' end credits and starting the National

Anthem early to catch those who were looking to get away immediately. The distinctive sound of the anthem's intro usually stopped them in their tracks and kept them fixed to the spot until it ended.

Any ideas of things like telephone cold calling, junk mail, email, credit cards and Internet shopping and banking would have been pure science fiction in the 1950s. Instead, we had door-to-door salesmen selling everything from insurance to the *Encyclopaedia Britannica*, and tallymen selling all sorts of goods for 1 shilling a week on the never-never. In the 1950s, the postman would deliver letters and postcards twice a day and each morning the milkman would deliver milk to every house on the street; each wore a smart uniform including a shirt and tie and a peaked cap. Our parents paid for gas and electricity in advance through 'shilling in the meter' boxes that were fitted in our homes. Most people didn't have a bank account and so workers were generally paid in cash at the end of each week, sometimes on a Thursday. This meant that the majority of purchases were paid for in cash, including all the routine household bills. All of the main services and goods suppliers had local offices or shops where you could go to pay your bills in cash. People didn't need to have a bank account; many preferred to put their savings in a Post Office account and buy postal orders for any payments that had to be sent by post.

Healthcare was nowhere near as advanced as it is today and we lacked the benefits of modern-day medical treatment, but the healthcare system we did have seemed very efficient and somehow more personal than it is today. The National Health Service was still in its infancy, having only been formed a few years earlier in 1948, and there seemed to be much less red tape than there is nowadays. It was very easy to see a doctor when you were ill and there was no need to make an appointment to be seen at the surgery. You only had to ask for a home visit and the doctor would be there the same day, seven days a week; they would even come out in the middle of the night if required. Of course, the population was much smaller in the 1950s and so there was less pressure on the health service, but there were a lot of chronic and incurable diseases to contend with and medical care was much more labour intensive, especially in hospitals. From a patient's point of view, the hospital nurses seemed to be much more hands-on in the wards and they had much less administration to contend with.

There were no prescription charges in the early days of the National Health Service, but this was later reviewed and in 1952 a charge of 1s per prescription form was introduced together with a flat rate fee of £1 for any dental treatment. In 1956, prescription charges were reviewed again and thereafter patients had to pay 1s for each item that appeared on a prescription form.

The overall pace of life in Britain was much slower than it is today, with buses and bicycles being the most popular modes of transport. In 1952, there were no motorways in the UK and only 2.5 million cars on the road (compared to 26 million in 2011), with most working-class families relying on public transport for any long journeys. We frequently walked rather than use buses, and the majority of schoolchildren walked to school on their own each day. Street crime was quite low and we felt it was safe to walk the streets, even at night. The total number of all crimes recorded by the police in 1952 was about 10% of the number reported in 2010. People were more inclined to report crime back then because the police were more likely to investigate anything that was reported to them. It was also quite legal for anyone to carry a knife and it was common practice for young schoolboys to have a penknife in their pocket, but such penknives were regarded as tools rather than weapons. Children had great respect for their elders but at the same time their disciplined upbringing also made them slightly fearful of adults, especially of anyone in authority. You never heard stories of old ladies getting mugged in the street for their pension money. It would have been hard to comprehend such a wicked crime being carried out back then. As young kids, we were all told not to talk to strangers but we never heard of any children being abducted. We would secretly carve our initials into tree trunks and on park benches, but there was no such thing as graffiti as we now know it and there was very little else in the way of vandalism. Mobile phones didn't exist and few people had a telephone installed at home because it was really expensive to have one and it was considered a luxury item. They would normally only be found in business premises and in some well-off households. The majority of people used public telephone boxes when they needed to make a call and for most that was not very often, the preferred method of communication being letters and postcards. If you did need to use a telephone then you rarely had to walk far to find a public phone box; when you did, the telephone would be in working order with a pay-box full of pennies and not looted. Each box was fully glazed with a light inside so you could read the telephone directories that were stored next to the telephone. The boxes were completely enclosed and weatherproof with heavy spring-closing doors, and they were capable of holding two people (or six kids as all baby boomers will know). Inside, they may have smelt a bit musty or damp but there was no smell of urine and you were very unlikely to find anyone sleeping in them.

As children, we spent as much time as possible playing outside in the fresh air and we were quite healthy, but we still got all of the usual childhood illnesses and we lived in fear of catching dreadful diseases like polio, diphtheria and tuberculosis (or TB as it was generally known). There was no such thing as children's rights and we were expected to obey any rules that were imposed upon us without question. We were taught that children should be seen and not heard and it was common practise for us to be physically punished for any wrongdoings, and not just by our parents; anyone in authority, such as a policeman or park warden, would give us a clip around the ear if they caught us up to mischief. Most of the painful beatings were done at school as corporal punishment was still lawful, and teachers were allowed to used various flogging tools to beat you with, including the traditional school cane and a leather strap with its serious end split into a number of tails to provide that extra-painful whipping action; some favoured the use of a slipper, but the cane was the thing that was most commonly used in schools, especially in England.

The children we grew up with came from families who shared the same cultural background as ourselves. They most likely grew up in the same local area as we did and their families had probably lived in the same district for generations before. The country had a rich mix of regional traditions and customs and people were proud to boast their own distinctive local accents. It was very easy to tell what part of the country someone came from by the way he or she spoke. Similarly, the British people had a recognisable identity at home and abroad. People from other nations found it easy to recognise and describe the British, albeit the image of us was sometimes over caricatured. The country had always been a magnet for immigrants and refugees from all over the world, but 1950s Britain was not the multicultural society it is today. Immigrants had previously come to Britain in relatively small numbers and so the population remained overwhelmingly British-born, white and Christian. There were, however, a fairly large number of baptised Christians who were non-churchgoers and non-believers. As a consequence, many 1940s baby boomers went right through their childhood without coming into contact with anyone from any other ethnic group, even in some of the most densely populated inner city areas. This was probably due to the fact that immigrants tended to feel more comfortable living among people from similar cultural backgrounds as themselves and so they would form their own communities in specific areas of large cities. People of different races didn't tend to mix very much except when work brought them together, otherwise preferring to stay within their own communities. This suited most of the white indigenous population who were quite apprehensive about immigration and not too keen to encourage integration. There was a lot of suspicion and discrimination born out of a fear that the increasing numbers of West Indian and Asian immigrants would steal other people's jobs by working for lower pay. At the time, there were no racial discrimination laws in existence and some businesses and individuals openly discriminated against certain groups of people. Discriminatory notices like 'No Irish. No Dogs' were already a familiar sight outside boarding houses and these were rewritten in the 1950s to read, 'No Irish. No Blacks. No Dogs,' and in some areas Jews were also added to the list of unwelcome patrons. With more and more non-white immigrants coming into the country, the feeling of hostility towards the Irish began to soften and the discriminatory signs were modified to read, 'No Blacks, No Dogs.' Some public houses operated a straightforward colour bar by displaying signs brandishing the words, 'No Blacks'. All women of any colour or race were also discriminated against in more subtle ways, mostly relating to employment, but in other areas as well, such as in obtaining membership of clubs and getting credit facilities. To get something on credit or hire purchase terms, a man was usually needed to act as guarantor, preferably their husband. It was also considered unladylike for a woman to go unaccompanied into a pub, but this was more to do with respect for women rather than discrimination.

In the 1950s, Britain was still a nation of manufacturers and shopkeepers with more than 70% of the British working population doing hands-on manual jobs. It was the heavy industries like coal mining, iron and steel making, ship building and engineering that were the big employers and more than 9 million workers were members of a trade union. There were plenty of jobs around and the majority of people who wanted to work had full-time jobs. Those who were working usually got one week's paid holiday each year and it was up to the employer to determine when that holiday would be taken. There were only 178,000 men and 64,000 women receiving unemployment benefit, compared with 1.01 million men and 483,700 women in May 2011. There were another 100,000 people registered as being unemployed who did not qualify for benefits under the 1946 National Insurance Act. Some of these were unable to work because of disabilities or sickness, and there were others who were only classed as short-term unemployed.

Many of our young dads would have been earning less than £10 a week for working a basic thirty-nine-hour week (the average weekly wage for men was £9 in 1952, which was worth about £200 at 2009 prices). Most of our mothers would have stayed at home to bring up the children but if they had gone out to work they would have been paid just over half a man's wage for doing the exactly same job. Dad might well have worked in one of the thousands of factories or workshops that stood on every corner of every street, at a time when Britain was a manufacturing nation capable of filling our flourishing high street shops with every kind of British-made product imaginable. He almost certainly walked or got the bus to work, stopping at the corner shop to buy a packet of cigarettes and his morning newspaper before he set off. Whatever kind of job he did, manual or clerical, his workplace would have been bustling with other workers, with no sign of a computer or any other labour-saving technological device. As the breadwinner of the family, Dad would expect to find his dinner already cooked and on the table waiting for him when he got home from work. Sadly for 1950s women, the advent of the 'modern man' was still some years away, which meant that after he had eaten his dinner the man of the house would retreat to his favourite armchair to read the newspaper while listening to *The Archers* on the wireless, and mum would be left to wash up the dishes.

We may have been very young children at the time but many of us still have vivid memories of life in the early 1950s. During those tender years, most of us lived in our mother's shadow, generally getting under her feet while she tried to keep the house in order. Less than 10% of under-5s went to nursery school (compared to 90% in 2011); the rest of us stayed at home with mum. The full-time mothers were unable to go out to work, but once their children started school many got themselves part-time jobs for a few hours a day. However, such jobs were hard to come by because the working hours had to fit in around the school day and it was almost impossible to juggle part-time work with looking after the kids during school holidays. Traditionally, ordinary families regarded it as the mother's duty to personally care for her own children and to nurse them through the early stages of their development. Mum was expected to be the main source of influence over her children, especially in the pre-school years. Dad had his role too, but many working dads saw too little of their children. We virtually lived in mum's pocket and it was her we relied on for guidance. Even if there had been an abundance of free nursery schools all over the country, it is unlikely that the average 1950s mother would have used them. The idea of leaving a child in a nursery all day so that mum could go out to work and earn money to improve the family's living standards was out of kilter with the 1950s way of life. The upper classes were well practiced at being separated from their children through the use of nannies and boarding schools, but everyone else thought it was wrong to separate a child from its natural mother for long periods at a time. Our stay-at-home mums were called housewives and they seemed quite happy with that tag, regularly describing this as being their occupation when asked. A housewife had a very demanding role to fulfil; it was hard physical work because there were no labour-saving devices in the typical family home and many of the daily chores were energy sapping. By the end of the decade, less than a third of households in Britain had a washing machine and these were single tub, top-loaders with a wringer on top. There were a small number of high street launderettes in existence but they were hard to find and very expensive to use. Most people still did all of their washing by hand and the average family with three children created lots of washing, scrubbing and ironing. These laundering jobs were done in-between all of the cooking, baking, sewing and everything else mum had to do.

The wartime practice of 'make do and mend' continued for many years after the war ended, which meant that when mum wasn't knitting a cardigan or making a dress, she was darning socks and altering hemlines to fit growing children. She also had a constant battle with surface grime, which was produced from a combination of cigarette smoke and solid fuel emissions. The popularity of open fires meant that she also had the fire grates to clean out each day. Because there was no fridge in which she could keep perishable foods, Mum also had to find time to do a daily shop for fresh dairy products and other groceries. With so much dusty manual work to do during the day, housewives usually wore a wraparound housecoat or an apron to protect their clothes from getting stained. However, it was quite normal for a housewife to wear good clothes around the house so if anyone knocked on the door she could throw off her apron and look respectable when greeting a visitor.

Those of us who enjoyed the pleasure of having younger siblings will remember the smell of damp nappies around the house. Our young mums seemed to spend hours at a time washing endless numbers of terry towelling nappies that had been generously soiled by our younger siblings; she would then boil them in a big pot on the stove before pushing them through a hand-operated mangle and hanging them on the outside washing line. In rainy weather, the clean wet nappies would be hung in front of the open fire to dry, thus adding to the damp conditions that many of us remember from our childhood. We had none of the modern-day building materials that we all take for granted today. Home improvement and weatherproofing products like double-glazing, sealants and insulation materials were not available. The man of the house usually did any basic home decorating and repair work that needed doing, and some men would occasionally undertake larger home-improvement projects, but most houses remained cold, draughty and damp in winter.

A few years down the line, our generation would be credited for introducing most of the home comforts that ordinary working people now regard as essentials in their homes. No modern-day home comfort was more welcomed by the baby-boomer generation than central heating, but we would have to wait another ten or twenty years before it would be affordable for the average family. Many of us are still haunted by memories of the cold winter nights of the 1950s.

The healthy, home-cooked food we pushed around our plates at dinnertime didn't seem to put an ounce of flesh on us. We used up so much energy while playing outside in the fresh air that most of us remained as thin as rakes no matter how much we ate. We really felt the cold and in wintertime we were well practiced in the art of shivering. The only source of heat usually came from an open coal fire in the main living room where the whole family would huddle together during the long, dark winter evenings. Windows and doors were mostly ill-fitting and heavy curtains were needed to stem the strength of the cutting draughts that whistled through every tiny crack. Rugs would be jammed under the internal doors and bits of screwed-up newspaper stuffed into keyholes to stop the flow of cold air breaking through from the unheated hallway. In the absence of a suitable curtain, a thick blanket would be hung across the main street door to stop the outside, sub-zero temperature from entering the house. Even when the living room reached a nice cosy temperature and you were warm enough to remove your hand-knitted pullover, you still had to keep a woolly jumper to hand in case you needed to venture outside of the snug living-room cocoon and into a cold area of the house. Such movement would be avoided at all costs; even if you were dying for a wee-wee you would cross your legs and hold on to it for as long as possible, rather than face the prospect of having to go out into the winter weather to use the freezing cold outside lavatory. At bedtime, you would make every excuse under the sun to delay moving your nicely toasted legs from the fireside to brave the chill of your frosty bedroom. When you did finally surrender to the inevitability of having to go to bed, you did so in your stockinged feet and at breakneck speed, hopping across the carpet runners and skidding along any bare bits of exposed lino. The bedroom was as unwelcoming as it ever was on winter nights; as chilly as the outside air and with draughts coming from all directions. Your panting warm breath turned into clouds of fog as it met the bedroom air. With no time to spare, you quickly got ready for bed, skipping across the bedroom floor in time to the rhythm of your chattering teeth, and swiftly diving under the bedcovers to find the shelter that your body so desperately craved. You would then fully bury your head beneath the tightly packed blankets and sheets. Despite your mum's best efforts to pre-warm the bed with a hot water bottle, the sheets would still have an icy, damp feel about them. Still shivering underneath the bedclothes, you would begin to sense the early stages of a thaw within your bones as the heat from the hot water bottle at the foot of the bed started to penetrate your thick woollen socks and gradually warm the soles of your feet, bringing your legs back to life. The warm puffs of breath you directed up your nose would produce small droplets that would fall from the end of your frozen nose. You knew that it would not be long before you would have to bring your head out from underneath the bedcovers, otherwise you would suffocate from the weight of blankets, which were topped off with a thick heavy overcoat to act as a poor man's eiderdown. You would pray that your whole body would soon be warm and that you would fall asleep before the hot water bottle turned to ice. In next to no time, your trembling would subside and you would become motionless, away in the Land of Nod, dreaming of all the fantastic adventure games you could play if you were to wake and find the streets basking in warm sunshine. The reality of morning always came too soon and the bedroom temperature was always as cold as it was the night before. To make matters worse, frost would form overnight on the inside of the bedroom window and the damp atmosphere was made worse by your warm breath as it created condensation that ran down the window and formed pools of water on the windowsill. Such memories do not feature amongst our fondest and are high on our list of things we don't miss about the 1950s; nor do we miss having to wash in a tin bath by an open fire, or having to use an outside lavatory. It is only a privileged few who can say that they never experienced the cold, draughty and damp living conditions that were commonplace before central heating, home insulation and airtight windows and doors were fitted in our homes. Unfortunately, most of us had to wait until we were much older before we were able to experience the great luxury of living in a warm home with hot and cold running water and an inside loo.

Many of us had not yet reached the primary school age of 4½ when the 1951 Festival of Britain took place. At the time, it was Britain's grandest and most important post-war event. London had already hosted the 1948 Summer Olympics (an event that became known as the Austerity Games due the economic climate of the time) and the Festival of Britain was intended to be an all-embracing affair: an event that the whole country could experience. It was intended to show how the country was recovering and rebuilding after the war and to give the people a feel-good boost while at the same time promoting the very best of British design, science, art and industry. There were Festival of Britain exhibition sites in all of the main cities around Britain and many of us went to visit one with our parents, albeit as bewildered infants. The most popular visitors' sites were in London, with 8.5 million people visiting the South Bank site, which included The Royal Festival Hall and some temporary South Bank attractions, like the Dome of Discovery and the Skylon. These had all been specially constructed to act as the centrepiece of the festival. Also in London, the Festival Pleasure Gardens in Battersea proved to be very popular, attracting 8 million visitors. The festival started on 3 May 1951 and lasted for four months. There were organised street parties all over the country, with bunting and Union Jacks proudly displayed everywhere. Many of us were too young to fully take part in the festivities but we enjoyed waving our flags and we had our fair share of fruit-flavoured jelly.

The Festival of Britain celebrations may have bedazzled us infants, but those four months of festivities were dull in comparison to the street parties we held to celebrate the coronation of Queen Elizabeth II on 2 June 1953. Because of the post-war baby boom there were now many more young children around and so there were a lot more street parties, and they were much bigger than those we had seen during the Festival of Britain. We were now old enough to take a full and active part in the celebrations. Some of us were fortunate enough to be among the 3 million people who lined the pavements of London to see the newly crowned Queen's procession pass by, while others crammed themselves into the living rooms of their wealthier neighbours to watch it all on newly installed 12in television screens. It was the first time ever that a monarch's coronation had been televised for all to see. Those who couldn't get to see it on television had the option of either staying at home to listen to a commentary on the radio or going out to one of the various public-viewing venues that had been set up in places like cinemas, church halls and hospitals. Cheerful celebrations took place in every nook and cranny of the country and even the rain didn't dampen the atmosphere. Once again, the nation showed its great patriotism with brightly coloured displays of red, white and blue flags, and bunting criss-crossing streets and market squares throughout the nation. Children wore lots of different homemade fancy dress outfits and many donned replica royal crowns made out of cardboard. There was also lots of specially printed coronation merchandise, including paper aprons, bibs, napkins, mugs, games and picture albums. For many of us, the Queen's coronation was probably the most memorable event of our entire childhood.

At the time of the Queen's coronation, most of our parents were in their mid- to late 20s but to us kids they seemed much older. Many had signs of worry and hard work etched into their faces and few dressed at all fashionably, often wearing the same type of clothes our grandparents wore. Although it was by now less common for men to habitually wear hats and raincoats, it was still popular practice for them to wear a collar and tie at all times, even when pottering in the garden or mowing the lawn; 1950s men didn't seem to do casual dress. In summer, women would wear brightly coloured dresses and sandals but the men would still don their usual shirts and ties. Many continued to wear their demob suits every day for years after the war had ended. The hairstyles and clothes of the day also made people look much older than their years. Few carried any excess bodyweight, with most people being on the thin side, and this only added to the older look.

Starting primary school was the first real milestone in our young lives. The occasion broke many hearts and brought about major changes to our daily lives. We were forced to completely alter our daily routine and we had to learn to get through each day without mum's help. It was a very stressful and confusing time for us; suddenly torn from our mother's apron strings and from the safe comfort she provided at home during the day. It was the start of growing up and there were so many things we would miss. We were waving goodbye to the wonderful taste of Farley's Rusk biscuits and the thick syrupy welfare orange juice we loved so much; these would soon be just a memory to us. Fortunately, as growing children, we would need to keep taking our daily spoonfuls of Virol malt extract, and most of us thought that was l-o-v-e-l-y. The bad news was that we had to continue with our daily dose of that awful-tasting cod liver oil. There were also some new unwelcome tasks that we would have to contend with at school, like the frequent inspections carried out by the school's 'nit nurse', and the humiliation of regularly stripping to our underwear and standing in line to wait for our routine medical check-up, which was done by the school doctor. We had to quickly adjust to the discipline of school life because there were lots of rules to obey and these were strictly enforced. The teachers did adopt a gentle touch when dealing with the infants in their charge but there was no pampering or fussing over any of the sad-eyed new arrivals, not when the teacher had forty-plus infants to manage. Fidgeting and whispering were the teachers' main enemies in the classroom and you soon learnt to sit still, be quiet and pay attention. There was no sign of any cuddly toys or any hint of an afternoon snooze. Punishment for misbehaving in class soon progressed from being made to stand in the corner to a slap across the back of the legs with the flat edge of a ruler.

During the Monday class register call we would hand over our tightly protected 5-bob school dinner money to the teacher. The kids from poorer families stood out from the rest because they were never called up to pay their dinner money and it was obvious to the other children that they were getting free school meals. We had a school assembly each morning when we were told of any important things that were happening, like special church services, new rules we had to obey or things we were doing wrong. We would also say prayers for the starving children in Africa and the people suffering in Soviet-occupied eastern European countries like Hungary and Poland. At mid-morning on every school day we would each get a small (⅓ pint) bottle of free school milk to drink. The majority of us liked the free school milk but not in the freezing cold of winter when we were made to drink it even when the bottles felt like blocks of ice.

School uniforms were commonplace and again the rules were usually strict, even in infant school. The uniforms for primary school were designed to be unfussy and affordable, and mums found that by shopping around on the high street they could put most outfits together. Girls commonly wore a white blouse, grey gymslip or pinafore dress and a lightweight summer dress. White socks and the regulation navy blue knickers were always evident and girls never wore trousers to school. Boys would wear white or grey shirts and grey flannel trousers with long, grey woollen socks. Most schools had a school blazer, mainly for boys, and some schools made the children wear caps and bonnets as part of their uniform. It was normally mum's job to sew the school badge onto the breast pocket of the blazer and on the front of the school cap or bonnet, but sometimes a metal badge would be pinned to the front of a girl's bonnet instead. Everything to do with the frugal fifties was practical and sensible, so there was no room for fashionable footwear at school. We all wore heavy, black leather shoes or boots that were indestructible and designed to last a lifetime. When holes did start to appear in the leather soles, dad would apply a pair of Phillips' stick-on soles in the hope that the shoes would last another ten years, during which time one of the younger siblings might also get some use out of them. We had nothing like the designer trainers that have become essential everyday wear since the 1970s. Our only shoes of comfort were the black canvas plimsolls we all had, but these were not designed to take much in the way of kids' daily rough and tumble and so they were generally only used for school games or PE.

At infants' school we were taught to recite the alphabet and we were shown how to do some basic arithmetic using an abacus. We also learnt how to write short words with chalk on a small, hand-held blackboard. Our teachers read stories to us and we sang lots of nursery rhymes and did loads of drawings and paintings. We were taught how to make easy things using a few basic materials and we learned how to co-ordinate our movements through dance and games. We played loads of throwing and catching games with small beanbags, and we learnt how to kick a ball in a straight line. After spending a year or two in the infant school we moved up to primary school and began to mix with the big kids. By the age of 6, we were using pencils to write, rather than the early learning tools of blackboard and chalk, and within a very short time we were being taught how to write with pen and ink. However, we used a crude type of pen not much better than the old feather quill pen; it was made out of a short wooden stick with a metal nib fixed to one end. We each had an inkwell fitted into the top right-hand side of our desks (we were all expected to be right-handed) and we would dip the nib into the inkwell to load it with enough ink to write a couple of words at a time. The nibs were not at all reliable in controlling the flow of ink and the pages in our exercise books would get covered in splodges of ink, as would our hands. It was very messy and a difficult task to master. Some kids never managed to get the hang of it, always getting more ink on themselves than on the page.

The post-war baby boom meant that there were a lot more families with young children in the 1950s, and families tended to be larger in number than they are today. Accordingly, schools had to accommodate lots of pupils, especially in urban areas, and so it was normal to have a large number of pupils in each classroom (often more than forty to a class and just one class teacher to teach them; there was no such job as classroom assistant in those days). We did loads of creative things like drawing, painting and model making, and we practiced singing a lot. The classrooms usually had large loudspeakers installed high up near the ceiling so that we could listen to some of the 'Schools Radio' programmes that were broadcast back then. These included a weekly programme of sing-along songs, mostly sea shanties and the like, and we would all sing along to these using special 'Schools Radio' music books that contained all the words of the songs. The radio control switch was usually housed in a cabinet somewhere outside of the classroom in the central part of the school and we were regularly made to jump when it was switched on by mistake, blasting a sudden burst of loud noise into the otherwise quiet classroom.

The amount of exercise we got was not limited to what we did at playtime in the playground; we also did lots of PE, sport, swimming and cross-country runs, usually having to walk long distances to the school playing fields and the council-run swimming baths. We certainly did lots of non-academic things at primary school but we were left in no doubt that school was a place for learning. While we were taught the basics in science and nature, the main emphasis was on teaching 'the three Rs': a long-established term used to describe the skills of reading, writing and arithmetic. Our primary school education was always geared towards the ultimate life-changing test we would take in our final year at primary school: the 11-plus examination. The exam was in three parts: Arithmetic and Problem Solving, General English (including comprehension and an essay) and General Knowledge. As the name suggests, we did our 11-plus examinations when we were 11 years old. The results were used to determine which type of secondary school we were most suited to. The idea was that different skills required different types of schooling and there were three possibilities: grammar school, a secondary modern school or a technical school. If you passed the 11-plus then you were expected to go to a grammar school to follow an academic education, which might lead to you going on to university. However, passing the 11-plus did not guarantee a place at grammar school because there was an application process and this included at least one admission interview with the head of the school you were applying to join. Being rejected by three different grammar schools often resulted in the applicant having to go to a secondary modern school instead. Pupils who failed the 11-plus usually ended up going to a secondary modern school with the prospects of leaving school at 15 with little or no qualifications, unless they went on to a further education college afterwards.

As with everything about the 1950s, it is often the simple things that we remember most about our primary school years: the taste of aniseed balls and malted milk tablets we used to buy from the school tuck shop during mid-morning break; the enjoyment we got from swapping stamps, cigarette cards and coloured beads we used to keep in old tobacco tins; the fun we had modelling things with plasticine and papier-mâché; the awful cross-country runs we did in the rain and mud; the dreadful experience of using those brick-built lavatories in the playground. There are a thousand and one everyday things we remember about our 1950s schooldays, like the embarrassment of country dance lessons, motherly dinner ladies, paper-chains and party games, wooden pencil cases and leather satchels, conkers and marbles, and we can all remember shivering by the edge of the pool at the local baths while learning to swim. We can still picture the scene of young girls playing two-balls up the wall while singing skipping rhymes – 'salt-mustard-vinegar-pepper... '. We remember the disappointment of being cast in the role of 'second hump of a camel' in the Christmas Nativity play. Then there were all of the hopeful ambitions we never did achieve at primary school, like being made pencil monitor with extra responsibility for handing out the paintbrushes, and hoping we might get to play the tambourine rather than the triangle at the next rehearsal for the school orchestra. This small assortment of memories represents a tiny part of our overall primary schooling experience. We all had bad days that we would rather forget, but most of us tend to look back fondly on our early school years. Even those who disliked being at school will remember the contentment we felt in the shelter and safety of our classrooms on cold wet afternoons when our class teacher read short stories to us. The teacher would dramatise the action by using a different tone of voice for each character, just like a play on the radio. We were totally mesmerised by it and nothing could distract us from the plot. Perhaps they were the best days of our lives.

Whether we loved or loathed our time at school, we were always glad to get home when each school day ended, even if only to play outside with our friends. Home life was idyllic, quiet and unpretentious compared to the average family lives of today. As with our schooldays, the memories we retain from our childhood family life of the 1950s are frequently quite simple ones: the wonderful smells of mum's roast dinners and freshly baked cakes; the cosy nights we spent by the fireside listening to the wireless as dad snoozed in his favourite armchair and mum rolled a fresh ball of knitting wool from a skein stretched between a child's tiny arms; afternoon tea at auntie's, patiently watching the clock as mum caught up on all the latest gossip; Sundays spent at granny's, with talk of drawing rooms and parlours and aspidistra plants; an ashtray in every room and ticking clocks all over the house; rooms filled with brown wooden furniture and comfy armchairs stacked with lots of cushions, all engulfed in a heady mix of musty smells sweetened with furniture polish. Homes were so very different then; there were no flick-of-a-switch sources of entertainment except for the radio, but some of us had the added luxury of a wind-up gramophone and an upright piano; this, however, was the full extent of our home entertainment equipment and there were no fancy electronic gadgets to amuse us. People spent a lot of their leisure time at home reading, listening to the wireless or pursuing one of the popular hobbies of the day. Adult hobbies usually involved practical things to do with the home. The skills of needlework, knitting, darning, cooking and baking were handed down through generations of women and every mum seemed to be an expert and eager to show their daughters how to do it. Men were the gardeners and the fixers – anything that involved an engine or a hammer. As for us kids, when we weren't playing hopscotch or annoying the neighbours with games of 'Knock Down Ginger' and 'Tin Tan Tommy', we would be plaiting our plastic scoubidou strings or honing our yo-yo and hula hoop skills. We rarely got bored. Even if we were stuck indoors we would find something interesting to occupy us; whether it was reading books and comics, sorting through our collections of stamps and beads, or constructing something from one of the Airfix or Meccano kits, we always found a way to pass the time. In the evenings, families would often do things together, and not just at Christmas. Board games like snakes and ladders, draughts, Monopoly, and Ludo were very popular forms of family entertainment, and we would play loads of different cards games, from Happy Families and Snap, to Cribbage and Pontoon. We kids liked listening to the wireless as much as our parents and we especially enjoyed radio shows such as *The Clitheroe Kid*, *Dick Barton*, *Educating Archie*, *The Goon Show*, *Paul Temple* and *Meet the Huggetts*. Many of us begged to stay up late so we could listen to the scary science fiction serial, *Journey into Space*: the stuff that kids' nightmares are made of.

While teenagers hung out in coffee bars, youth clubs and dancehalls, we children burned up our excess energy playing in the local streets and alleyways, and on any piece of open land available to us. Many of our towns and cities still bore the scars of the Blitz bombing raids that left over a million houses destroyed or damaged in London alone. These bomb ruins and derelict buildings, together with all of the wasteland that was created through post-war slum clearance, became our natural playgrounds. We may have twisted a few ankles and got some bumps and bruises while playing amongst the hazardous rubble but we had some wonderful adventures, and the bomb sites provided the perfect place for us to build our bonfires each Guy Fawkes Night. We also came across an unexploded bomb or two and I suppose we should count ourselves lucky to have survived our childhood exploits.

We spent as much time as we could outside in the fresh air and memories of the long hot summers we loved so much are as indelibly printed in our minds as the cold, smog-filled winters we hated. It was a long time ago and some may think it's a trick of the imagination, but we did seem to have lots of warm summer days, when the morning lasted all day and we played outside until late into the evening. We had few toys but we managed to get a lot of enjoyment from what we did have, and we learned to share everything. If there was only one pair of roller skates or one bike then we would wait to take our turn or we would do without. We were experts at improvising and we would make our own playthings out of a few unwanted makeshift materials, often rescuing things from the rubbish. Everything had a use; cardboard, string, bits of wood and parts from a broken old pram were all put to work as valuable components for our home-made toys. From bows and arrows and toy guns to go-carts and sledges, we made them all. We would chalk stumps on a wall for a game of cricket and spend hours playing board games like Monopoly on each other's doorsteps. While boys played football in the empty streets using jumpers for goalposts, the girls would climb and swing from ropes tied to the tops of lampposts. All the girls delighted in playing dressing-up games using mum's make-up, frock and high heels, but neither boys nor girls had any real interest in fashion and we remained blissfully unaware of each passing trend. Girls were happy if they had a pretty ribbon in their hair, while boys would delight in having shoes without holes in them. We wore what our mothers dressed us in and for boys that often meant wearing the same clothes all the time, in and out of school. Girls generally fared better, usually having at least one other dress they could wear to play out in while their school uniform was neatly tucked away in the wardrobe. It was normal practice for young boys to wear short trousers until they started secondary school at the age of 11, but some would remain in short trousers up to the age of 12 or 13. Sometimes the move up to long trousers was determined by how quickly you grew out of your last pair of short ones; people were prudent with their money and were only inclined to discard clothes when they were worn out and could not be mended any more. Parents also had very different ideas about the way children should be brought up, with many seeking to prolong the childhood of their little darlings for as long as possible. It was much easier in those days to protect a child's innocence because they were not being seduced by adult themes at every twist and turn in their lives. Sex was rarely discussed in the home and there was no sex education whatsoever at school. Celebrity idols of the day always dressed and behaved modestly in public and there was no risk of children ever hearing bad language on the radio or television. Children were not exposed to any sexual images in magazines or on street hoardings as they are today, and there were no agony aunts writing about sexually explicit matters in any of the publications we read. Most of us learned the facts of life by exchanging snippets of knowledge in the school playground and reading rude postcards on day trips to the seaside. The absence of any proper sex education didn't lead to an uncontrollable spread of venereal diseases among the young and we didn't see any pregnant 13-year-old schoolgirls in the 1950s classrooms. Any influences the 1950s media had over children were usually harmless, apart from the tobacco adverts that portrayed smoking as being sexy and relaxing. The fact that we had little or no opportunity to travel outside of our own communities also helped to limit the amount we knew of how other people lived their lives; this meant that we were much less worldly wise than children are today. We were, however, given a great deal more freedom to roam the local streets and in doing so we learned how to assess situations and make decisions for ourselves, independent of our parents. Although we enjoyed a more lengthy childhood than you might expect today, being allowed out on our own without any supervision helped to make us streetwise from a very young age. Most of us walked to school unaccompanied each day and many of us were even allowed to travel alone on the buses and trains, reading maps and planning journeys for ourselves. Grandma's half-a-crown

(2s and sixpence) birthday money would often be spent on a child's Red Rover Ticket, which allowed unlimited travel anywhere you wanted to go on any of London's red buses. We may have been immature, scrawny young things but we were not completely naïve.

The austere times we grew up in taught us to be pennywise and enterprising. The little pocket money we were given was always inadequate and many of us used our wits to earn extra. The few child-labour laws that existed at the time were not properly enforced and so we were able to do various trivial and cheap-labour jobs even though we were underage, from helping the milkman on his early morning round to shunting boxes around in the markets at weekends. Some of us did the traditional early morning newspaper rounds while others used their initiative to create entrepreneurial money-making jobs like selling coal door-to-door from an old pram. In those days, nobody was interested in saving the planet and everything went into the dustbin, but 1950s kids were experts at recycling and we made money by rummaging through dustbins to find stuff we could collect and sell to the local scrap merchant: everything from old newspapers and cardboard to rags and bits of metal. We specialised in collecting empty beer and lemonade bottles and returning them to the off-licence to get back the 3d a bottle deposit that people had paid when they first bought them. Nothing we did made us rich but it gave us a few extra pennies to spend and it broadened our education. We may have only earned enough to pay for our ticket to get into Saturday morning pictures, to buy a comic and a few sherbet lemons, but it taught us the value of money and we learnt that nothing in life is free; that is if you don't count the odd Saturday when we used to bunk in the cinema through the exit doors at the back.

We grew up in the midst of a 1950s rebellious youth culture that was enacted mostly through the dress and activities of Teddy Boys, Beatniks and Greasers. Weapons of violence such as flick-knives and knuckle-dusters were openly displayed and sold in high street shops and there was no age restriction on who could buy them. We did not feel at all threatened by their presence and we still felt safe walking the streets, even after dark. The bad behaviour of angry and unruly teenagers, however, was usually bought into line when they were called up to do their compulsory two years of National Service at the age of 18. Prior to this, teenagers would hang out in any public place that had a jukebox installed, from coffee bars to skating rinks. The radio stations only played a limited range of music and playing jukebox records was about the only way young people could get to hear the latest music loudly and with good quality Hi-Fidelity sound (Stereophonic sound from 1959). During the 1950s, jukeboxes started to be manufactured to take the new style 7in 45rpm vinyl singles and each machine could take up to 200 record selections. They, especially the Rock-Ola and Wurlitzer jukeboxes, fascinated everyone; groups of people would stand around them to watch the coloured lights and the automatic record-changing mechanism. Teenagers would push each other out of the way so they could be next to put their money in the coin slot and choose their

own favourite records at a cost of sixpence a play or three for
1s. If you didn't like the record that was playing then a sharp
thump on the side of the machine would dislodge the needle
and an automatic arm would lift the record off the turntable
and return it to its filing slot at the back of the machine; the
next record would then be played. This was the cause of many
a fight.

We may have only been in our pre-teen years but we still
shared in the thrills and excitement that surrounded the
ground-breaking films and record releases. They heralded
the arrival of what was to become the biggest ever change in
popular music culture: rock and roll music and the acrobatic
rock and roll version of 'lindy hop' dance that came with it. It
arrived from America in the mid-1950s, pioneered by artists
like Bill Haley and his Comets, and Elvis Presley the 'King
of Rock and Roll'. Around the same time, we began to hear
recordings of a new style of British skiffle music, which had
started in London's basement jazz clubs through bands like
Ken Colyer's Jazzmen and in particular his banjo player at the
time, Lonnie Donegan. At last we had some new exciting music
we could listen to as an alternative to the crooners, balladeers,
jazz and big show bands of old.

The advent of rock and roll and skiffle music coincided with
the welcome demise of the cumbersome 12in 78rpm shellac
gramophone records and the arrival of the new 7in 45rpm
single vinyl discs, and we were told that we would soon be able
to buy records that we could play in two-channel stereo sound
if we had a suitable stereo player. To us, this stereo sound

innovation seemed light years away and it was well beyond our short-term expectations. We remained content to dream that one day we might be able to have one of the most desired and 'must-have' machines of the 1950s: the British-made Dansette portable mono record player with a built-in speaker. Just a little while later, in 1957/58, those of us lucky enough to have a television set were able to watch some of the new popular music shows that were beginning to be broadcast by the BBC for the very first time, shows like *Six-Five Special* and *Oh Boy!*. These shows featured live performances from new and up-and-coming artists like Cliff Richard, Petula Clarke, Marty Wilde, Billy Fury, Tommy Steele, Shirley Bassey and the popular balladeer Ronnie Carroll. Most television screens only measured somewhere between 9in and 14in and they all produced a 405-line grainy black-and-white picture that appeared on the screen in tones of silvery grey. We had to sit up close to the television screen to see all of the action, and the sound was awful. It was also useful to sit within touching distance of the television set so that you were close enough to land it with an almighty whack on top of its cabinet to settle its picture whenever it went haywire, which was a regular occurrence because television reception was very poor in the 1950s. But this was our first opportunity to see live rock and roll performances in our own front room and so we thought it was great. Music lovers fondly remember the 1950s as being the heyday of rock and roll music, but even at the height of its popularity the British record-buying public remained loyal to home-grown heart-throb ballad singers like Ronnie Hilton,

Michael Holliday, Dickie Valentine, David Whitfield and Jimmy Young. We were still captivated by all sorts of soppy love songs, and British female artists like Alma Cogan, Shirley Bassey and Ruby Murray all managed to compete well against rock and roll artists in the popular music charts; as did lots of American, male and female artists such as Pat Boon, Nat 'King' Cole, Perry Como, Bing Crosby, Doris Day, the Everly Brothers, Guy Mitchell, Johnnie Ray, Frank Sinatra and the very popular Canadian artist Paul Anka. However, in terms of music phenomena, the 1950s probably belonged to Elvis Presley – even though Frankie Laine had more UK top ten hit singles in the 1950s than Elvis (nineteen against Elvis's eighteen, each having four UK number ones). We kids had scores of our own special favourites too, including lots of novelty tunes, like Max Bygraves' 'When You Come to the End of a Lollipop', Mandy Miller's 'Nellie the Elephant', and the two popular Danny Kaye songs, 'Little White Duck' and 'The Ugly Duckling'; these were all played regularly on *Uncle Mac's Children's Favourites Show*, which we listened to each Saturday morning on the BBC Radio's Light programme, *Hello children, everywhere!*.

Being just children at the time, we were touched and sometimes bewildered by some of the events that made headline news during the 1950s. The death of King George VI on 6 February 1952 left its mark on us because everyone was so upset and the whole country was in mourning for days afterwards. Immediately following the announcement of the King's death, BBC Radio cancelled all of its usual programmes and played solemn music for the rest of the day. It was a Wednesday and a normal school day for us kids, but we were still caught up in all of the grieving because our teachers were openly saddened by the news and there were long faces everywhere you looked; everyone was in a state of depression.

In May 1953, we were all excited by the news that Edmund Hillary and Sherpa mountaineer Tenzing Norgay had become the first climbers known to have reached the summit of Mount Everest in the Himalayas. Most of us had no idea where Mount Everest was apart from the fact that it was thousands of miles away, somewhere on the other side of the world. Our geography lessons at primary school didn't stretch as far as Nepal and China. A year later, in May 1954, we were all very impressed when we heard that the English athlete, Roger Bannister, had run the first ever sub-four-minute mile. It seemed an impossible achievement to us kids who were struggling to do 100yds in half-a-minute. We all wanted to have a go at doing the four-minute-mile but most of us lost all interest after we had been running for about fifteen-minutes and the end of the mile was still nowhere in sight.

An event that was to prove of great benefit to us children of the 1950s and beyond was Parliament's introduction of a Clean Air Act in 1956. This was important to us because it sought to address the problem of air pollution and to stop the dense fogs that regularly engulfed us in horrible yellowish smog, especially in London and other highly populated industrial areas. These smogs were commonly known as 'pea-soupers' because they had the consistency of thick pea soup. The smog was caused by cold fog mixing with coal fire emissions and many people died from the effects of breathing the polluted air. London's Great Smog of 1952 left more than 100,000 people ill with respiratory problems and some of these died prematurely as a result. The Clean Air Act legislated for zones where smokeless fuels had to be burnt and it identified power stations that needed to be relocated to rural areas. The winter air quality was much improved in subsequent years.

Up until 1956, we had only known a life of peace; we had heard all of the stories of war from the older generation but we had grown up in a wholly peaceful Britain with no fear of terrorism or war. However, there was a short pause in our hopes for long-term peace when news of the Suez Crisis began to dominate the newspaper headlines in October 1956. Britain, France and Israel invaded Egypt in an attempt to regain Western control of the Suez Canal after Egypt nationalised the Anglo-French Suez Canal Company, intending to finance a dam project using revenue from the canal. Fortunately, due to the intervention of the first United Nations peacekeeping force, the conflict only lasted a matter of days, which meant that Britain could once again return to its previously calm state.

In 1957, we read that a European Economic Community (Common Market) had been established between the six European countries of Belgium, France, Germany, Italy, Luxembourg and the Netherlands. The idea was for these members to promote peace and economic growth through cooperation and trading agreements. It didn't affect Britain;

we would continue to row our own boat and to conduct our worldwide trading relationships as a sovereign state, managed entirely by our own elected government. In fact, it was unlikely that Britain would ever join the EEC because the British Government would never surrender any of its powers to a European bureaucracy.

In July 1959, as we sat in our local cinema waiting to see Marilyn Monroe in *Some Like It Hot*, we were shown a film in the Pathé News of an amazing hovercraft skimming across the English Channel; what would they invent next? In November that same year, many of us went to see the Alfred Hitchcock film, *North By Northwest*, and on that occasion the Pathé News included the launch of the new Morris Mini Minor (the Mini) at October's Earl's Court Motor Show. At the same time, Pathé News featured a film of the newly opened first section of the M1 motorway, which ran between Watford and Rugby. Britain's first ever motorway (the Preston Bypass, later to become part of the M6) had been opened a year earlier in 1958. The new M1 motorway promised no traffic jams and it looked as though that would be the case because you could see from the Pathé Newsreel that the motorway was almost completely empty. After all, there were still less than 5 million cars on Britain's roads at the time. Surprisingly, there were no speed restrictions on this new motorway and motorists could go as fast as they liked. In those days, the average family car struggled to reach 70mph, so it was only the high-powered motorcars and motorcycles that could take full advantage of this new no-speed-limit superhighway. Some over-ambitious drivers managed to blow up their engines while trying to achieve high speeds that were beyond their cars' capabilities, and there were no MOT vehicle tests back then, so any old banger could take to the roads.

The unpretentious lifestyle of the 1950s now seems quite primitive, but we lived very active and healthy lives and most of us enjoyed our childhood even though we had very little money and few possessions to shout about. Our unsophisticated upbringing helped to mould a generation of unspoilt children, or as close as you might get to one. In fact, it was probably the last decade in which children were allowed to grow up slowly and truly enjoy the benefits of a carefree childhood. Most managed to retain their childlike innocence right up to the start of their teenage years and often beyond. Those childish, fun-filled years were uncorrupted by television, gadgets and electronic communications. They were innocent, fun years and we were very lucky. We were content with our lives in those austere childhood years, albeit though inexperience and ignorance, but as we reached puberty we became more and more eager for change. We developed ambitions of our own and we craved a better way of life: one that resembled the sophisticated images we regularly saw in films and on television. Those brief glimpses into a celluloid world of heady carefree opulence helped demonstrate how it might be possible for us to leave the sober 1950s mood behind us as we moved into the next decade. This baby-boomer generation would go on to become the 1960s teenage revolutionaries and the cultural innovators who would shake up the world and steer the country through the latter part of the twentieth century and beyond.

three

From Gymslips to Miniskirts

New Year's Day 1960 arrived without any special fuss. In Scotland it was a Bank Holiday, as it had been since 1871, but it was a just a normal working Friday for everyone else. We celebrated the ending of the old year and the start of the New Year in just the same way as we had done on every other New Year's Eve. There was nothing at all remarkable about the occasion. We didn't open our eyes on New Year's Day 1960 to find that the 'swinging sixties' had arrived and that we were now living in a new and modern world of carefree hedonism. There was no sudden change in the nation's opulence or attitude; in fact the crossover from the 1950s to the 1960s was a seamless and unexciting event that passed without any fanfare to mark the dawning of what was to become a very special decade, and even more so for us, the younger generation.

At the beginning of the 1960s there were plenty of jobs around but the post-war economic recovery was an on-going process and there had been no obvious changes in the way working families lived their lives. Back in the mid-1950s, we had seen how much the birth of rock and roll and skiffle music had livened up an otherwise staid generation of post-war underprivileged teenagers, but since then there had been a lull, with little happening to get young people excited. Most of us were still living a meagre 1950s lifestyle in cold houses that were filled with brown furniture, and we still thought it was only the posh that had indoor lavatories. For many of us, the thought of having hot running water was just an unattainable dream, and even more so was the idea of turning one whole room of a house into a washroom that would be fitted with just a sink, a cast-iron bath and nothing else. What an extravagant waste of space! As yet, the old kettle-filled fireside tin baths had not been completely consigned to the scrap heap and the local municipal bath houses were still doing good business, charging people sixpence a time to have a bath. At least we didn't have to suffer the indignity of wartime bathwater rationing when whole families had to make do with just 5 inches of bathwater once a week to be shared, one after the other. We had moved on a bit since the war; several years had passed since the days of rationing and you could now have whatever you wanted, as long as you could afford to buy it. However, living standards were still relatively poor, as were the conditions that many people had to put up with in their workplace. Fashions were also stuck in the 1950s with winkle picker shoes and beehive hairdos. Heart-throb singers like Adam Faith, Emile Ford and Anthony Newley continued to dominate the popular music charts. Nothing much had changed at all.

Fortunately, there were some young and talented entrepreneurs who were starting to make their mark on London's fashion scene with some great, innovative ideas. Working independently of each other, trendsetters like Mary Quant and John Stephen had been among the first to open new-style clothes boutiques in London's West End in the mid-1950s and the unusual clothes they sold were by now proving to be hugely popular with fashionable young Londoners. Word of their success was now starting to spread far and wide. With Quant specialising in womenswear and Stephen in menswear, the ground-breaking work that these two young people did in the late 1950s and early 1960s created a style of fashion that would later become a major part of 1960s mod culture; it would completely transform British fashion, kick-starting the post-1963 'Swinging London' era that focused the world's attention on London's Kings Road and Carnaby Street. While Quant and Stephen were busy building-up their fashion empires, a number of other talents were also doing their bit to close the door on the seemingly dull 1950s. These included two people who were to become pioneering icons of the sixties and beyond: Vidal Sassoon and Terence Conran. Vidal Sassoon is the man who everyone associates with 1960s geometric hairstyles and his success allowed him to open the first worldwide chain of hairdressing salons. But, in the early 1960s, he was still experimenting in his Bond Street salon with his own unusual new cuts and techniques in hairdressing and was unknown to the wider world. Meanwhile, Terence Conran was designing and manufacturing ranges of furniture in ground-breaking, modern styles that were aimed at the new generation of young 1960s homemakers. Unfortunately, it was going to take another couple of years before the new wave of mod fashions would really take off around the country, and we youngsters would have to wait just as long for the next new dance craze (The Twist) to arrive from America and liven us all up. Even then, we could not envisage the cultural changes that lay ahead of us.

The summer of 1962 came and went and still there were few people outside of Liverpool and Hamburg who had heard of a group called The Beatles; their first hit single record, 'Love Me Do', had not yet been released and there was absolutely no sign of any Beatlemania. The drab 1950s mindset of the early 1960s gave us no hint of the home-grown cultural revolution that was about to take the whole country by storm, but by the mid-1960s, London would be dubbed the fashion capital of the world and the city would become known as Swinging London, as defined by *Time Magazine* in 1966. Subsequently, the same 'swinging' tag would be used to describe the period from around 1963 until the end of the decade: forevermore known as the 'Swinging Sixties' era. It got this label because it was in those years that we saw the most noticeable move away from Victorian values and the birth of what was called the 'permissive society', when attitudes to everything seemed to become increasingly liberal. There was indeed a more relaxed attitude to sex and sexuality and a more liberal approach to all forms of censorship. Abortion and divorce were also made easier and we saw the end of capital punishment. It was also in the mid-1960s that the second wave of feminism emerged and members of the Women's Liberation Movement burned their bras in the street and demanded equality.

Meanwhile, back in the pre-1963 days, before even the modern bikini had become popular beachwear in Britain, our main focus was still on school life. The early 1960s period was an important time for us because we were now at secondary school and having to deal with all of the teenage moodiness and acne that came with our newly acquired youth status. We were maturing in body and mind and our social and intellectual interests were beginning to change. This was a confusing time in our lives when we had to absorb all sorts of different information in a short period of time and our future career paths would be determined by the amount of knowledge we absorbed at secondary school. It wasn't easy because we were now at an age when we were most open to distraction and it was so easy for us to lose our concentration. Teachers would regularly hurl objects across classrooms to regain the attention of daydreaming students; pieces of chalk and blackboard rubbers were among their favourite missiles. If a teacher was within reach of someone who was not paying attention then a swift clout across the back of the head would quickly remedy the situation. With so much going on in our young minds, it was hard for us to focus solely on our schoolwork, especially during double Latin or English literature lessons on hot summer days. Our heads were filled with muddled thoughts of everything from nuclear bombs to sex. Some of us were beginning to show an unusually keen interest in literature, eager to get a peek at one of the illicit copies of the banned book, *Lady Chatterley's Lover*, which were being passed from satchel to satchel in school playgrounds up and down the country in the early 1960s.

As the months went by, we found we were using the playground much less for play and more for idle chatter. We began to find the younger kids around us irritating and childish; we were now part of the older brigade – too cool to play games. Amazingly, we began to fill our entire break times discussing all sorts of trivial issues, from what happened on *Coronation Street* the previous night to who was number one in the latest pop-record charts (or *Hit Parade*, as it used to be called). It was also in the playground that we picked up most of our knowledge about sexual matters. We would swap snippets of information about things we had heard or read and we would tell one another rude jokes. There were some weird and wonderful stories about sexual matters and there was always a lot of brave talk going on, but few had actually experienced any kind of sexual activity at that young age. When all the talk was done, each of us was left to sort the fact from the fiction as far as sex was concerned. There was no sex education at school in those days and it was usually a taboo subject at home as well.

With our newly acquired coolness came the temptation for us to start smoking cigarettes, a sure sign of being 'cool' and mature; an image we saw depicted on advertising hoardings on every street corner. It was all part of growing up and most of us felt we had to try it at least once. Many were sick after their first puff and gave up immediately, but there were plenty of others who carried on smoking and unintentionally began a lifetime of nicotine addiction. You needed very little money to get hooked on smoking because most sweet shops sold cigarettes in packets of five and some even provided a special single-cigarette service for young school kids. These shopkeepers would break open a packet of cigarettes and sell them in singles at 3d each. Children and teenagers usually bought Player's Weights Cigarettes or an equivalent because they always seemed to be the cheapest and it didn't really matter to us what the brand was – a cigarette was a cigarette. You would regularly see schoolchildren smoking in the street when travelling to and from school; they would even smoke at break times when they were at school. There wasn't the stigma attached to smoking back then. You were supposed to be over 16 to buy them over the counter but the rules were very relaxed. There wasn't any publicity about possible health risks; in fact the advertising campaigns gave the impression that cigarettes made you feel better, calmed you down and made you relax, hence the 'cool' image. All of the older school buildings had outside lavatory blocks and these were used as hideouts for smokers during break times. Teachers and prefects would frequently make surprise 'smoker raids' on the toilet blocks to catch smokers at it. Innocent non-smokers would cross their legs and avoid going into the lavatory blocks for fear of getting caught up in a smoker raid and being wrongfully punished.

Desktop computers and the Internet were still decades away, and the word 'computer' was not yet used in everyday language. Even big computers were still in their infancy and in Britain they were only used in a few very large businesses. These commercial computers were huge – the size of a very large room – and they were a long way from being as sophisticated as the computers we now use. Technology was very primitive in comparison to today. Many of us still had no television or telephone at home and there were no such things as pocket calculators to help us with our maths at school. We had absolutely none of the modern-day information technology gadgets available to us; all we learned came out of books and we wrote everything down in books – no such thing as cut and paste in those days. Our school desks were crammed with all kinds of textbooks and we needed sturdy leather schoolbags or satchels to carry our homework books back and forth each day.

The way the schools were run and the methods of teaching were very different from today too. Each school would have a number of teachers who were qualified to teach in specific subjects and between them they would cover the whole range of subjects taught in schools. The type of school you went to would determine how many subjects you studied but it was usually around ten to fifteen. In a typical secondary school lesson, a teacher would stand at the front of the class and lecture the pupils on his or her specialist subject while chalking explanations and diagrams onto huge blackboards that were fixed to the front wall of the classroom. We also studied school textbooks and library reference books and we did enormous amounts of written work both in the classroom and at home, but the teachers' lectures were the principal method of teaching. At primary school, we learned to recite our times tables (multiplication tables) by rote and how to do simple arithmetic and mathematical problems. Now, at secondary school, we were expected to know our times tables by heart and be able to recite them on demand and to instantly calculate a specific multiplying task in our heads: Seven fours? Nine eights? Twelve sevens? We were also studying more advanced mathematics, including algebra and geometry. As a general rule, secondary-school children were required to use fountain pens for any written work and any mistakes had to be crossed out rather than rubbed out so that the teacher could see how you had arrived at your answers and where you had gone wrong in your calculations. We copied everything down in exercise books – a separate one for each subject – and we were marked on the standard of our handwriting and spelling as well as the quality and accuracy of our work. The range of subjects we studied was far reaching, including some things that we could never imagine as being useful to us in later life. There were some core subjects like maths and English that you had to continue with up to the normal school-leaving age of 15, but many schools allowed pupils to drop a few subjects as they progressed through the school so that they could concentrate more on their strongest subjects. This was especially the case for pupils who were intending to stay on at school until they were 16 to sit their General Certificate of Education Ordinary Level (GCE, O level) examinations. Unfortunately, in the early 1960s, not everyone was given the opportunity to take these exams. The majority of secondary modern schools did not cater for GCEs or any other alternative certificates of education. It was usually only the independent, grammar schools and sixth form colleges that provided for students to sit these exams. Up until 1965, when the Certificate of Secondary Education (CSE) was introduced, most secondary school children left school at the age of 15 without any qualifications at all. Prior to 1965, if they wanted to obtain any form of qualification they had to enrol for a further education course or join a sixth form college.

For the most part, secondary schools enforced strict discipline policies and any wrongdoing resulted in some form of punishment, included the writing of lines ('I must not...'). There were also a lot of after-school detentions and frequent use of corporal punishment (canings). You did hear stories of girls being caned or slippered but that was quite rare. Boys, on the other hand, were regularly beaten and sometimes for fairly minor misdemeanours. It was often the independent and grammar schools that imposed the toughest rules of discipline and administered the harshest punishments to those who dared to break them. Some schools even had designated punishment rooms where offenders would be caned during their lunch break or after school. It was also not uncommon for boys to be caned in front of their classmates and sometimes in front of the whole school. Such public canings were usually reserved for major offences, such as bringing the school into disrepute, fighting in the street or barging in front of an old lady at the bus stop. In schools where corporal punishment was used, teachers would carry a cane around with them, usually secreted beneath their clothing (many wore gowns), and they would lash out at the first sign of laziness or wrongdoing. Schools were supposed to register each punishment they meted out in an official 'punishment book', but these were never kept up to date and there are no proper records to show how much beating actually went on. Some of the physical punishment was quite brutal but the threat of it was often all that was needed to maintain discipline. There were plenty of playground scraps and rivalry between neighbouring schools, especially among the boys, but there was no graffiti or vandalism and few cases of theft, and you very rarely heard of anyone being expelled. Some schools chose not to use any form of physical punishment for misbehaviour, opting for gentler forms of chastisement instead. This was more prevalent in all-girls schools and mixed-sex schools where the same types of punishments would apply to boys and girls alike, with a leaning more towards writing lines, walking around the playing fields after school and detention. These kinds of penalties were also handed out at the schools that used corporal punishment but only in cases of minor rule breaking; the preferred option was to beat the wickedness out of you.

In state schools, it was quite normal to have between forty and forty-five pupils in each classroom, but teachers still managed to command silence during lessons and we would never dare speak to the teacher without first putting up our hand and waiting for them to give us permission to speak. Teaching was a highly respected profession and teachers always dressed formally to look the part. Some were softer on discipline than others and, as children do, we sometimes tested their patience to the limit but we remained respectful of their position. We always stood up whenever a teacher entered or left the classroom and we would address teachers as sir or miss; there was never any familiarity between students and teachers.

When moving around the school, we had to walk in single file, never run, and we were expected to keep silent while in the school buildings. Outside of school, we were told that we must never walk more than two-a-breast along a pavement and that we must stand aside to allow anybody coming from the other direction to go past. If we were travelling to school by bus or by train, we had to give up our seat to any adult who was left standing, especially pregnant ladies, the elderly and anyone with a disability. Many schools banned pupils from leaving the school premises at break times unless they had written permission to go home for lunch. We were expected to use the lavatories during break times and not to have to ask to go during lessons. This could prove difficult because of the problem with smokers commandeering the toilet blocks at break times, but we had to manage. At the end of the school day, before we left our classroom, we would check the area around our desks and pick up any litter that may have been accidentally dropped during the day and then we would stand our chairs on top of our desks in readiness for the cleaners to come in.

As we grew into young teenagers our school uniform became an embarrassment to us, more so for those with brightly coloured or unusual uniforms. We began to feel very self-conscious about our appearance and what made matters worse was that our young teenage years coincided with the start of the 'Swinging Sixties' period, when it suddenly became very important for us to be fashionable, whatever our gender. We were now too cool for gymslips, hockey sticks, school caps and blazers. We began pushing the boundaries of school uniform rules: altering blazers by removing the coloured braiding and unpicking seams to make fashionable vents; boys removed turn-ups from their trousers while girls rolled up the waistbands of their skirts to make them shorter. Everyone tried to get away with wearing stylish shoes instead of the ugly regulation school shoes, commonly known as fish-boxes. We were becoming rebellious teenagers and there had never before been a better excuse for rebellion because we were the teenagers of the 1960s and this was turning into the most exciting decade ever.

As far as popular culture is concerned, the period from 1960 to 1962 was a fairly drab time. During those first two years of the 1960s we did see some changes in popular music and fashions but nothing really remarkable. In 1961, at the age of 14, singer Helen Shapiro took the country by storm when she became the youngest ever female chart topper in the UK with her number one hits, '*You Don't Know*' and '*Walking Back to Happiness*'. Around the same time, the record producer Joe Meek was busy creating his now-renowned 'Wall of Sound' style of popular music from his legendary home studio above a leather goods shop at 304 Holloway Road in London, where he produced number one hits for John Leyton with the haunting '*Johnny Remember Me*' and The Tornados' '*Telstar*', which turned out to be his most famous work of all. We called rock and roll and pop bands 'groups' back in the 1960s, and groups like The Rolling Stones, Manfred Mann and The Dave Clark Five had already formed and were starting to develop large numbers of fans around the London area. At the same time, Liverpool was already revelling in their very own Mersey Sound with groups like The Beatles, Gerry and the Pacemakers and The Searchers. Indeed, every city in the UK seemed to be generating its own crop of home-grown popular music talents. Among these up-and-coming bands of the early 1960s were The Hollies, who were working the clubs in their native Manchester, and The Animals, who had already amassed a large following of fans in their hometown of Newcastle-upon-Tyne.

By 1962, Jacqueline Kennedy, the wife of President John F. Kennedy, had been hailed as the fashion icon of the 1960s, appearing on the front cover of every newspaper and magazine throughout the world. We were fairly content with life as it was in the pre-1963 era because we knew no better, but in hindsight there was nothing special going on culturally and little to excite us brand-new teenagers. The most significant social activities available to us at the time included an evening down at the local youth club and the occasional church hall dance. Those of us who were tall enough and brave enough might sometimes sneak in to see an X-rated film at the local flea-pit cinema. Our main access to pop music was through the staid BBC Radio service and in the evenings we could listen to the commercial broadcasting station, Radio Luxemburg. The trouble with Radio Luxemburg was that most of the country got very poor quality reception and there was a constant problem with hissing noises and fading sound. We were always twiddling with the tuning knob, trying to get a better signal. It seemed like the only bits you could always hear clearly were the incessantly repeated adverts for Horace Batchelor's secret Infra-Draw method for winning the football pools. Our choice of television viewing was also limited. We just had two channels, BBC and ITV, and we had to watch our favourite shows on 405-line small screen monochrome analogue television sets. The pop records we bought at the time were only available as mono recordings, but that didn't matter too much because no one had a stereo record player anyway and we had never experienced anything other than mono sound. 'The Twist' dance craze kept everybody happy on the dance floor but other than that we were still struggling to break free from the aura of the 1950s. The best-selling single of 1962 was Acker Bilk's 'Stranger on the Shore', and Frank Ifield's 'I Remember You' followed close behind. We certainly needed something revolutionary to happen to shake off the dust and get us post-war baby boomers going.

We did occasionally step outside of our self-obsessed teenage bubbles to follow world events. We all took a great interest in news reports of the space race developing between Russia and the USA. Back in 1961, we were amazed to see the Soviet cosmonaut Yuri Gagarin becoming the first human to orbit the earth in outer space on board the *Vostok 1* spacecraft. We saw regular news reports of the Vietnam War and we were all very pleased that Britain showed no signs of being drawn into the conflict. However, when the Cuban Missile Crisis started on 14 October 1962 it seemed possible that the Cold War, primarily between the USA and the USSR, was getting closer to becoming a nuclear war, and this frightened us all, especially British teenage boys who were fearful that the government might bring back conscription, which had only ended a couple of years previously, on 31 December 1960. We knew that if the government were to reintroduce conscription then all of us post-war baby boomer boys would have been called up when we reached the age of 18 and sent off to war. Mind you, we also knew that we might not be around long enough to celebrate our 18th birthdays if there was to be a nuclear war. Fortunately, the Cuban Missile Crisis was short-lived and a joint agreement to resolve the situation was reached on 28 October 1962, thereby allowing all British teenage boys to rest easy again and get back to more important personal issues, like combing our hair and looking cool. We had grown up in a peaceful country and this was the closest we had ever come to knowing the fear of an impending world war. Thankfully, we were now able to return to our previous state of calm to await a more welcomed disturbance that would begin to happen in 1963, heralding the arrival of the exciting period of the 1960s that we all look back on so fondly. It was in that year that 20-year-old Jean Shrimpton hit the headlines and became the face of the sixties, knocking Jacqueline Kennedy off all of the magazine covers. At the same time, the new 'mod' fashions were being sold in a growing number of London boutiques and these mod styles were starting to appear in national magazines; the mod culture was spreading countrywide. This year was the turning point when everything seemed to be changing from lacklustre to brilliant and The Beatles were among the front-runners of this new-wave cultural movement. Their 1962 single release, '*Love Me Do*', only reached number seventeen in the UK record charts, but they were now on the verge of greatness and about to start their long domination with the release of '*Please Please Me*' as an A-side single. That was in January 1963, and we didn't know it then but we were witnessing the birth of what was to become known as Beatlemania. Very soon, the eyes of the world would be on England and everyone would want to come here and visit places like Liverpool and especially London, to feel its special atmosphere and be a part of the liveliest and most trendy place on earth.

These cultural changes coincided with some very noticeable improvements in the majority of people's overall standards of living. At long last, we were starting to have baths and toilets fitted inside our houses and we were filling our homes with lots of modern household conveniences, or 'mod cons' as we called them: from washing machines and fridges to central heating and instant hot water supplies. Gradually, we were having all these luxurious things installed in our homes, albeit decades behind the Americans. We were even getting our own personal telephones installed by the GPO (General Post Office) and in two-tone colours as well. Mind you, in the 1960s the demand for telephones was so great that many of us had to put up with sharing a telephone line with a neighbour; it was called a party-line, which meant that two or more subscribers shared the same pair of wires and only one party could make a call at a time. It was a terrible service but at least we had our own telephone, which meant we no longer needed to use the draughty public telephone boxes out in the street. Foreign holidays were also starting to become more affordable, enabling some of us to replace our annual week in Clacton-on-Sea with a trip to the sun-drenched Costa Brava. Suddenly, our living rooms were being adorned with lots of naff souvenir ornaments from all over Europe. Bob Dylan and Joan Baez-style folk singers became commonplace entertainers in coffee bars up and down the country and a new type of 1960s live music began to bellow out from high street pubs and basement clubs all over the place.

We delighted in being able to see all of our new-style 1960s pop idols perform at the local town hall and cinema venues, and at affordable prices. Whereas today it is common practice for pop concerts to be held at large venues like the O2 Arena or Wembley Stadium with one main act and a support act, in the 1960s a pop concert would be staged very much like one of the reunion tours that take place today; the most likely venue would be a cinema rather than a stadium and the concert would usually include half a dozen top recording artists of the day. For example, The Beatles first Christmas show at the Finsbury Park Astoria in London also featured Billy J. Kramer & the Dakotas, Tommy Quickley, The Fourmost, The Barron Knights, Duke D'Mond, Rolf Harris and Cilla Black. There were two performances each night, at 6.00 p.m. and at 9.00 p.m., and ticket prices were 5/-, 7/6 and 10/- (5s, 7s and sixpence, and 10s). Unfortunately, the sound system, stage set and lighting were nothing compared to what is available today but the atmosphere was electric; we had never seen or heard anything like it before. The Beatles were lowered onto a brightly lit stage in a fake helicopter, which was considered to be amazing at the time and a real break with tradition. The concerts back then may not have been the slick, huge-budget shows we have today but they were much more intimate. The fans could actually see the stars of the day up close. We could clearly see the beads of sweat on artistes' brows and there was no need to have giant screens showing the action because it was right there in front of us. The money-spinning merchandise business was still in its infancy in the UK and there wasn't any pressure on us to buy expensive printed t-shirts, albums and programmes. We didn't feel we were being ripped off and we had every chance of getting an autograph at the stage door after the show.

In the early to mid-1960s, we were leaving secondary school in our droves and many of us were still only 15. Most had opted to leave without any qualifications and yet nearly all managed to get fixed up some kind of job or apprenticeship fairly quickly. The rest stayed on at school to take O Level GCEs and some went on to take A Level GCEs (the highest school-leaving qualifications), but few went on to university. At that time, a university education was a choice reserved only for the upper classes and a few exceptionally clever middle-class academics. Some who were less academically inclined but who had good practical skills went on to further education in technical colleges or colleges of advanced technology, as they were officially known. In the early 1960s, the number of students in any form of higher education hovered around 200,000, only about 5% of the UK school population.

It was fairly easy for young school leavers to get a job when they left education. The newspapers were jam-packed with job vacancies. Many got themselves fixed up beforehand, often leaving school on the Friday and starting work on the following Monday. We had much greater ambitions and expectations than our parents' generation but we were still naive in terms of what a career actually was. Most saw ambition as wanting to earn as much as possible as soon as possible. Britain was as close to full employment as you could get, and whatever your age or qualifications, you were in with a good chance of a job. Mind you, you had to work hard when you got a job because these were the days when it was very easy for employers to get rid of you if you were lazy or no good.

There were restrictions as to the type of job you could get depending upon what part of Britain you lived in, and whether you lived in town or country areas, but jobs were plentiful and there was usually some overtime available to boost wage packets. Everything was still very labour intensive back then. There were no computerised production lines; instead, our factories were filled with workers and lots of them – more workers than machines. The situation was very similar in offices; they were often full to the brim with office workers and filing cabinets, and there were clipboards all over the place. Large companies would have several large, open-plan rooms to accommodate row upon row of typists and accounts clerks. Britain was still in the business of making things and it was fairly easy for a 15- or 16-year-old boy to get on some kind of apprenticeship scheme. Boys who wanted to become tradesmen could join a local firm as an apprentice plumber, electrician, bricklayer or whatever best suited them. Tradesmen were as the name implies, 'men'; these were not considered to be suitable jobs for women. Girls were still very much compartmentalised into certain jobs, such as shop assistants, machinists and typists, and they were still being paid less than men for doing the same type of work, but things were slowly changing for the better.

School leavers didn't command very high wages and for the first couple of years they were usually expected to act as general skivvies and gofers (go for this and go for that). Between the ages of 15 and 18, workers would get paid about £5 to £10 a week (most people got paid weekly then), but that would be enough for them to give their mum some housekeeping money, pay their fares to work, buy clothes and have a couple of nights out during the week. In the mid-1960s, a pint of beer cost about 1s 9d (about 8p in today's money). However, fashionable clothes were very expensive and teenagers usually had to save up before they could buy any new item of clothing; there were no TK Maxx or Primark stores in those days. Youngsters who wanted to keep up with fashion, like the 1960s mods, often bought their clothes on credit, paying a fixed amount each week. Alternatively, you could have something made-to-measure and pay it off weekly in advance before collecting it from the shop.

Young teenage workers usually lived carefree lives and fully enjoyed the mood of the 1960s, ever mindful of being part of a new, optimistic generation. We were fortunate to have been around at the right time as part of an increasingly affluent society. During our 1950s austere upbringing we were teased about there being a better life on the horizon but later we would be criticised for too readily grabbing hold of the opportunities that became available to us in the 1960s. As young people, we were fortunate to enjoy a long period of growing prosperity and spend much of our young lives without the burden of a major economic recession. We made the most of it at the time, but we will be forever criticised for having done so. There will always be some blinkered political pundits looking to brand the baby boomer generation as the luckiest and most powerful generation the world has ever seen. We will be criticised for enjoying what will come to be described as the selfish excesses of the 1960s, and it is likely that we will be blamed for everything bad that ever happens in the world forevermore.

The television period drama series, *Heartbeat*, which ran from 1992 to 2010, was a wonderful, nostalgic look at sleepy village life in Yorkshire back then, but it didn't show anything resembling the true mood of the 1960s. And where did they get those clothes? A sleepy country village where three policemen have time to investigate every reported case from a broken window to a lost dog, and a local doctor who pops around to see all and sundry to cure everything from pimples to runny noses; it might be said that the *Heartbeat* series didn't even reflect what rural village life was like, let alone the whole mood of Britain in the 1960s. However, it was gentle and enjoyable to watch – just a drama series; pretend; make believe; not reality. The true atmosphere of the 1960s pulsated through towns and cities across the country, especially London – the heart of everything, the centre of all the action and the driving force behind the whole 'Swinging Sixties' phenomenon. London was indeed the music and fashion capital of the world. From Kings Road to Carnaby Street, the West End pavements were heaving with visitors looking to feel the vibe and be a part of what swinging London was all about. The decade overflowed with a wealth of originality and style in every aspect of life, from the E-Type Jag to the Mini car, from Twiggy to Quant, from The Rolling Stones to The Beatles, from Radio Caroline to Radio London, from mods and rockers to the hippies, from the Marquee Club to The Scene, and from *Thank Your Lucky Stars* to *Ready Steady Go!* We had protest singers, peace movements, women's lib and even space exploration. We had everything and it was all happening in the 1960s.

The cultural explosion of the 1960s has left an indelible mark on the memories of those of us who were lucky enough to have been around at the time, and we continue to reminisce fondly of those heady days. Fifty years down the line, the post-1960s generations continue to show great interest and fascination in the music, fashions and events of the decade that is still affectionately known as the 'Swinging Sixties'.

I grew up in 1950s London, where we were spoon-fed a diet of rock and roll music through movies, radio, specialist magazines and the BBC's ground-breaking television shows *Six-Five-Special*, *Cool For Cats*, *Oh Boy!*, and *Juke Box Jury*. It was all very exciting for us post Second World War, baby boomer kids, but nothing was to prepare us for the avalanche of eclectic styles of music that were heading our way as we moved through the early '60s. We had no idea how much our lives would change and we never expected the decade to provide such great experiences. I remember the springtime of 1960, being holed-up in a coffee bar and sharing one bottle of Coca-Cola with half a dozen of my mates while listening to the Everly Brothers' song, 'Cathy's Clown', being repeatedly played on the jukebox. I recall the heavy thump of the needle hitting the record and the scratchy bass sound as it made its way across the record's grooves to the start of those unmistakable first few haunting bars of that song. I also remember the beautiful sound of The Percy Faith Orchestra's instrumental, 'Theme from a Summer Place', which often echoed around the walls of the same coffee bar. I was approaching the gateway of my teenage years without knowing that this was to be the best ever decade in which to be a teenager.

The miniskirt, The Beatles and the E-Type Jaguar immediately spring to mind when recalling icons of the 1960s, but they were just the icing on the cake. The decade was crammed full of special people and events that would forever be regarded as symbols of the 1960s. England won the football World Cup in 1966 and we have revelled in that glory ever since, but at the time we didn't fully appreciate and celebrate the achievement as we would if England won it today; there was so much else going on in 1966. This was a very special time, a period of social, economic and political history that will always be fondly remembered, and the music and fashions of the 1960s will always be admired. From the mini skirt to the topless swimsuit, the 1960s revolutionised twentieth-century fashions, and many items have survived the test of time and still remain at the height of fashion. There are also lots of 1960s singer/songwriters, including Bob Dylan and Paul McCartney, who are still recording and entertaining us today.

The 1960s were all about war and peace, and everything in between; from the Vietnam War to flower power and the summer of love; from the twist to the locomotion, and from the Mersey Sound to blue beat, the 1960s were never boring.

'If you can remember anything about the sixties, you weren't really there,' is a famous quote by Paul Kantner, the American psychedelic rock musician. However, there are still many people around today who did manage to get through that magical decade without succumbing to the drug-fuelled dream world that scrambled the minds of some. Yes,

I remember the sixties and I was really there; it was a great time to be a teenager living in London. To borrow a couple of lines from Mary Hopkin's hit song of 1968 (English lyrics by Gene Raskin), 'Those were the days, my friend! We thought they'd never end. Those were the days. Oh yes, those were the days!'

four

Kipper Ties, Shagpile and Discontent

It was very sad having to wave goodbye to the 1960s, and for many of us the saddest moment of all was waking up on New Year's Day and having to face up to the fact that we were now in the 1970s. We really did believe that the atmosphere of the 1960s would go on forever. At the very least, we expected the mood to carry on into the next decade, but end it did, and as if in an instant, pretty much everything changed and we baby boomers came down to earth with a terrible bump. There were certainly plenty of clues around in the late 1960s to show that our sense of fashion was starting to wane when we began flirting with things like hot pants, tie-dyed shirts and frayed bell-bottomed jeans. Women had taken to wearing brightly patterned, polyester jumpsuits, sometimes referred to as hostess pyjamas, with culottes-style of flared leggings, and there was even a short-lived craze for women's disposable paper knickers. However, there were a number of late 1960s fashion disasters that went on to become very popular 1970s fads. Many of these would have been regarded as cringeworthy in the mid-1960s but they were perfectly suited to the new wacky world of hotchpotch 1970s style. The new-wave fashion gurus of the 1970s were keen to have a style revolution that would be as ground-breaking and far-reaching as the 1960s one had been. We certainly saw some strange sights on our streets during the 1960s but none so strange as we were about to witness in the 1970s world of all things weird and wonderful. All at once, we seemed to lose any sense of style and good taste and we appeared to be oblivious to what was happening. Our trend-setting teenage years were now just distant memories and we became feeble followers of fashion rather than the leaders we once were. Perhaps we just lost interest in it all and stood back to allow a younger generation to make their own sweeping changes as we had done ten years before. Whatever the reason, surely us baby boomers cannot be held responsible for the succession of embarrassing outfits and styles that paraded our streets during the 1970s. Yes, we did succumb to wearing such things as kipper ties but only because it was hard to find anything else in the shops at the time.

The clean-cut hairstyles of the 1960s were abandoned and we allowed our hair to grow excessively long. Men's hairstyles now ranged from the perfectly cut, blow-dry look to that of a neglected shaggy dog. There was also a lot of strangely sculptured facial hair, which did nothing to improve the image of the 1970s man. We also began to see exaggerated versions of the mullet hairstyle emerge, similar to that worn by Tom Jones for a period in the late 1960s. Although the style didn't reach the peak of its popularity until the 1980s, the likes of David Bowie and Paul McCartney proudly sported this short-top-and-sides and long-at-the back mullet cut during the 1970s. As always, women did their best to be creative, using large rollers to shape and create volume in the hair, then landscaping it with all sorts of lacquered flicks and curls. Later in the 1970s, women tended to use much less lacquer and hairstyles became more free-flowing and wispy in appearance, typified by the three girls in the 1970s *Charlie's Angels* television series. The large Afro-style, ball-shaped hairdo was very popular among black men and women and many black entertainers adopted the style to its extreme, as with some members of 1970s pop groups, like The Jackson Five and The Stylistics. The miniskirts of the 1960s remained fashionable throughout the 1970s, thank goodness, but flashing back to what we remember of the 1970s fashion revolution tends to evoke less-favourable images: things like the aforementioned kipper ties and the snug-fitting tank-tops that were matched with colourful bell-bottomed ankle-swingers that looked down on peculiar-looking platform shoes. As far as fashion was concerned, the 1970s could be described as the era of 'big hair and big flare'. We were exposed to the extraordinary sights of glam rock with men in makeup, and punks who wore safety pins and spiked collars as jewellery. There was also a nationwide army of Bay City Roller fans who wore tartan ankle swingers in homage to their pop idols. The period is commonly referred to as 'the decade that style forgot'. A little harsh perhaps, but some of those 1970s fashions were simply unforgivable, and for that reason it might be wise for us to keep our old photograph albums hidden away in a dusty corner of the attic where nobody is likely to find them.

We certainly had peculiar ideas of what looked good in the 1970s, and this peculiarity was not restricted to the clothes we wore. We acquired an all-round tasteless streak that affected our ability to distinguish between what was chic and what was tacky, and we managed to combine these two features to create an overall impression of bad taste. We began to decorate and furnish our homes differently, with trendy geometrically patterned wallpapers, glass-topped chrome tables and yards and yards of shagpile carpet. Our homes were awash with all shades of purple, orange and brown. We became obsessed with the colour brown; from bedspreads to curtains, we just couldn't get enough of it. We ripped out the traditional white enamelled, cast-iron bathtubs and replaced them with new mass-produced, lightweight acrylic ones. We could now buy complete bathroom suites in all sorts of colours, from the reddish purple of maroon to avocado shades of green, and of course chocolate brown was one of the most popular colours. The bathroom was no longer seen as just a utility room – a cold wash place that we nipped in and out of as quickly as possible. It was now a room in which we could spend time and relax while pampering ourselves with fragrant bubble baths and splashes of Brut cologne. We installed heating in the bathroom, applied mirror tiles to the walls and we even laid fitted carpets – very chic but impractical and not very hygienic. We went on to create feature walls in our living rooms, which we clad in tongue-and-grooved pine panels, wood grain wallboards and cork tiles. The brown epidemic of the early 1970s quickly spread to our wardrobes and very soon we found ourselves dressed from head to toe in all shades of brown, and preferably in fabrics made from synthetic materials that would create a lot of static electricity to make our hair stand on end and surprise us with electric shocks when we touched something metal – it was the sparkling 1970s in more ways than one.

Many of us baby boomers may well be able to distance ourselves from the worst of the clothing fashion blunders of the 1970s because, by then, we were too old to get caught up in any of the extreme teenybopper crazes that came and went in the passing years. As long as those dusty old photograph albums never see the light of day then we can boast that we managed to resist the temptation of wearing any of those dodgy patterned tank tops, gaudy dungarees and flared satin trousers. We can unashamedly claim to have maintained our dignity and sense of style throughout the 1970s by dressing only in sophisticated and classic styles, which fortunately could still be found in some of the high street shops. In retrospect, it seems reasonable for modern-day critics to label the 1970s as 'the decade that style forgot', but at the time I suppose we all fell into the trap of thinking it was all very innovative and progressive. There was certainly nothing wrong in trendsetters trying to establish a special 1970s identity. Well, they did that all right!

A lot of the 1970s bashing is actually done tongue in cheek, but it is as well that we are a self-deprecating nation and by nature find it easy to laugh at ourselves; we can't really do much else when there is so much photographic evidence to show what 1970s Britain was like. Apart from the wonderful long, hot summer of 1976, which cheered our spirits, much of the decade was clouded in an atmosphere of gloom and we needed plenty of frivolous distractions to give us reasons to smile. Many people have grounds to look back fondly on the period and they will remember it as being a fun and exciting decade. These are usually the 1970s children and teenagers who were living at home with mum and dad at the time, and were too young to have first-hand experience of the serious side of the decade, with all of the associated unrest and hardship. We all like to think of our own childhood and teenage years as being the best of times and it is no different for the generation that grew up in the 1970s. This was before technological gadgetry began to dominate young people's lives; when youngsters were still very active and playing outside a lot. They played all the traditional games that we used to play and they had additional playthings that had been made possible through the skills of innovative designers using advanced manufacturing processes; from space hoppers to skateboards, they had a much greater choice of toys than ever before and they had plenty to occupy themselves. For the older kids and young adults, there was a lot going on in popular culture to provide enjoyment and help smooth their way through the years: from the seemingly innocence teenage pop idols like The Osmonds and David Cassidy to the larger-than-life singers and musicians such as David Bowie, Elton John and Queen, and of course Abba, the most successful musical act of the 1970s. We baby boomers might by then have been too dignified or perhaps too old to be seen shaking our booties around the disco dance floors, but we were young enough to appreciate the best of 1970s popular music and we have our own lasting memories of wall-to-wall funk and disco music. And then, in August 1977, we shed a tear and said goodbye to Elvis Presley, the King of rock and roll. His music had been a timeline in our lives and now he was gone. Very soon after Elvis' sad death, our hearts were cheered with images of John Travolta strutting his stuff to the sounds of The Bee Gees in the film *Saturday Night Fever*. Those dance floor images will remain etched in our minds forevermore. While the younger generation were absorbed in glam, punk rock and heavy metal, most of us baby boomers remained loyal to 1960s music, especially Tamla Motown, R&B and much of the Mersey Sound. We have to acknowledge that there was a lot of good new-sounding popular music around in the 1970s and the enormous catalogue now has an easily identifiable genre of its own. Even if you know next to nothing about popular music, you only have to hear a 1970s record on the radio and you can immediately recognise it as being from that era.

We should also credit the mood of the 1970s for having inspired talented filmmakers to produce large numbers of ground-breaking films. Many of the 1970s blockbuster films are now regarded as classics. There are far too many to mention them all by name but here a few of the noteworthy ones:

1970 – *Love Story, A Man Called Horse, MASH, Patton, The Railway Children, Airport.*

1971 – *A Clockwork Orange, Dirty Harry, The French Connection, Get Carter, Shaft, Straw Dogs.*

1972 – *Cabaret, The Godfather, The Poseidon Adventure, What's Up, Doc?*

1973 – *The Sting, The Day of The Jackal, The Exorcist, Live and Let Die, The Three Musketeers.*

1974 – *Blazing Saddles, Death Wish, The Towering Inferno.*

1975 – *Jaws, One Flew over The Cuckoo's Nest, Tommy.*

1976 – *The Eagle has Landed, Marathon Man, Midnight Express, The Omen, Rocky.*

1977 – *Close Encounters of the Third Kind, Saturday Night Fever, Star Wars.*

1978 – *Grease, The Lord of The Rings, Superman, Watership Down.*

1979 – *Alien, Mad Max, Monty Python's Life of Brian, Quadrophenia.*

The image we invoke of the 1960s being an exciting and colourful time is somewhat diminished by the fact that we had to view all of the televised pictures in black and white back then. The 1970s, however, brought colour television to the masses and with it came a number of hugely successful television shows. There were some wonderful 1970s comedy series and the best of them still entertain us today as they continue to be rerun night after night on television's 'Gold' channels. They include *Bless This House*, *Citizen Smith*,*Fawlty Towers*, *George and Mildred*, *The Good Life*, *The Liver Birds*, *Man About The House*, *On The Buses*, *Open All Hours*, *Porridge*, *Sykes*, *The Two Ronnies*, *Whatever Happened to the Likely Lads* and *Rising Damp*. We were also treated to another seven years of the much-loved *Dad's Army* series, and in 1973 we were introduced to the gentle humour of *Last of Summer Wine*. With all of that light-hearted comedy on offer, Morecambe and Wise still reigned supreme – and they were in colour!

There were a lot of innocent, fun programmes on television in the 1970s but there were also a number of controversial television comedy shows that were subjected to criticism by the renowned social activist Mary Whitehouse and the 'Clean-Up TV' pressure groups. There were several 1970s comedy programmes that were scheduled into early evening broadcasting for family viewing, which would now be considered offensive and politically incorrect: shows like *Love Thy Neighbour*, *Mind Your Language* and *Till Death Us Do Part*; not forgetting the highly politically incorrect 1970s stand-up comedy show, *The Comedians*, which featured the best nightclub and workingmen's club comedians of the day: comics such as Stan Boardman (famous for his anti-German jokes) and Bernard Manning, who managed to offend everyone but remained one of the most popular comedians of the day. Each episode of *The Comedians* was thirty minutes long and featured ten stand-up comedians taken from a pool of about forty. The show was peppered with lots of mother-in-law, racial stereotype and sexist jokes. Nothing seemed to be off-limits, even religion. This type of comedy was extremely popular at the time and *The Comedians* show was in fact so popular that it warranted two Christmas specials, went on several sell-out national tours and ran for a season at the London Palladium. It is amazing that having boasted such a following in the 1970s, it is difficult nowadays to find anyone who will admit to having ever found that style of comedy funny. How strange! Back in the 1960s and 1970s we thought Mary Whitehouse was a busybody and a spoiler of anything that could be labelled as being 'fun'. She seemed to want to ban anything that could in any way be linked to the 'permissive society'. Looking back on it now, perhaps she was not the spoilsport busybody we liked to think she was. Much of her clean-up mission now seems quite sensible and it could be said that she was right about many of the things she fought against, especially the unnecessary sex, violence and bad language that was being shown on our television screens at the time, and have become more commonplace in recent years.

In the 1970s, there was an abundance of good stuff on television, including a lot of new detective and whodunnit programmes, such as *Canon*, *Charlie's Angels*, *Columbo*, *Kojak*, *McCloud*, *McMillan & Wife*, *Quincy*, *Starsky & Hutch* and *The Sweeney*. Quiz and game shows were also really popular and plentiful too, with shows like *3-2-1*, *A Question of Sport*, *The Generation Game*, *Give Us A Clue*, *The Golden Shot*, *The Price is*

Right, *The Krypton Factor*, *Mastermind*, *Sale of the Century* and *Winner Takes All*. Our science fiction interests were satisfied with such things as *Blake's 7* and *Doomwatch*, and we saw the third and fourth doctors in the *Doctor Who* series, as portrayed by Jon Pertwee (1970–74) and Tom Baker (1974–81). We had classic serious dramas, such as *I Claudius* (1976) and *Jesus of Nazareth* (1977), and the very popular period drama series, *Upstairs, Downstairs*. Our weekly dose of popular music was provided by the likes of *Top of the Pops* and *The Old Grey Whistle Test*. Many baby boomers will also have fond memories of 1970s children's programmes, having sat down as young parents with their little ones to watch *The Adventures of Black Beauty*, *Tiswas*, *Multi-coloured Swap Shop* and *Bagpus*. We didn't go short of talent-spotting shows either, with *Opportunity Knocks* and *New Faces* providing plenty for us to consider. Indeed, it was the 1970s series of *Opportunity Knocks* that made household names of such stars as Little and Large, Peters and Lee and Pam Ayres. *New Faces* first came to our screens in 1973 and it introduced us to lots of would-be rising stars, including Michael Barrymore, Jim Davidson, Les Dennis, Lenny Henry, Showaddywaddy and the multi-talented and loveable Victoria Wood.

We watched a great deal more television than we did in the 1960s, partly because we were older and more settled stay-at-homes, and also because money was much tighter. We still had only three television channels to choose from (BBC1, BBC2 and ITV) but fortunately the restrictions on broadcasting hours were lifted in 1972 and we could now watch more television than ever before. We certainly had plenty to amuse and distract us from all of the doom and gloom that surrounded the industrial unrest of the 1970s. Those who were not seriously touched by all of the 1970s strife in the workplace might well look back fondly on the decade, and who can blame them for remembering the period as being the best time of their lives?

It was in the 1970s that many of us baby boomers first become truly independent, leaving the safety of our parents' nests and moving into the very first homes of our own. It was one of those great life-changing moments. Yes, at long last we had a place of our own and we were keen to decorate and furnish it in the latest 1970s style, with all the brown trimmings. Renting a colour television set was the first thing on the agenda with a trip down the high street to see what deals DER, Granada and Radio Rentals were offering. At that time, colour televisions were still fairly new to us in the UK and they were very expensive to buy and fairly unreliable too. As such, it was common practice for people to rent a television set rather than buy one outright. Hence, most of us did the rounds of all the high street television rental showrooms to see what was on offer. Once the television was sorted, we were then off to the nearest branch of Laskys to see the new Betamax video recorders in action and perhaps buy one of the latest Stereo 8, eight-track cartridge players with twin speakers, which would fit nicely into the new melamine wall unit in the lounge. There was no such thing as Internet browsing, online shopping and shopping malls back then and so we had to trudge the high street shops to see what was available and seek out the best deals for everything from a bar of soap to a three-piece suite.

Recent technological advancements had brought down the manufacturing costs of decorative-faced particleboard and the product was being used more and more as an alternative to real wood in the construction of furniture. Easy-to-clean and stain-resistant melamine-faced chipboard was becoming increasingly popular with the young baby boomer homemakers of the early 1970s and we delighted in filling our homes with all sorts of wall units and occasional furniture made from it. White melamine was by far and away the most popular colour but it was also available in several wood-grain finishes, much to the delight of those who wanted everything in shades of brown. We filled every alcove with books and records neatly stacked on row upon row of pre-finished melamine shelving (thank goodness for Contiboard). To complete the 1970s atmosphere, we needed to buy a stylish purple-and-orange lava lamp and at least one beanbag chair to go in the corner of the room. It was also fashionable to use spotlights to show everything off and to cast delicate shadows across the luxurious shagpile carpets. Essential accessories for the kitchen included a coffee percolator, wall can opener, electric carving knife and a Soda Stream carbonated drink-making machine. A new twin-tub washing machine would be nice if the budget would stretch that far, otherwise it would mean a weekly visit to the launderette. You might then need to save up for a new Goblin Teasmade machine for the bedroom; it was in the mid-1970s that they first began making them with built-in radio alarm clocks so you no longer had to wake up to the sound of an irritating buzzer noise.

Amazingly, having experienced the wonders of the Mini car and E-type Jaguar of the swinging sixties, we now longed to get our hands on weird-shaped new cars like the Ford Capri (with bright orange paintwork) and the Mark 3 Cortina (with yellow or mustard paintwork). We were captivated by the new car designs of the 1970s and we eagerly traded in our old Minis, 1100s and MGBs for the new Ford Fiestas, Morris Marinas and Triumph Dolomites. We even admired the new Austin Allegro car with its square-shaped steering wheel. In fact, we were more taken with the square-shaped steering wheel than the car itself. What happened to us free spirits of the 1960s, suddenly conforming to the eccentricities of the 1970s?

We baby boomers were no longer the carefree teenagers we once were. We were now in our 20s, all grown up and having to manage the responsibilities that came with adulthood, including raising children of our own. The fads and fashions that once consumed our lives were now just frivolous distractions from the main events of the 1970s. There were more important and serious things going on in the world, especially in Britain, and these events were impacting greatly upon our lives. The trivial goings-on of the 1970s only served to keep us sane throughout the madness of the endless industrial disputes and strikes that marred our whole way of life, and it was all happening at a time when most of us baby boomers were still fairly new to the experience of having to part with our hard-earned cash to pay the household bills and raise young families. To crown it all, we were being financially squeezed to death with the high rents and high-interest mortgages of the 1970s. It could be said that we were up to our necks in soiled nappies in more ways than one.

In the 1960s, we had seen inflation rise from just 1% in 1960 to a high of 5.40% at the end of 1969, but inflation really took off when we entered the 1970s and there seemed to be no way of stopping it. Driven by growth in government spending, increased oil prices, industrial disputes and higher pay deals, inflation in the UK got completely out of control in the 1970s, averaging 13% a year. By the end of 1975 it had reached 24.20%: the highest we had seen it go in Britain since the First World War. Young baby boomers who had taken out mortgages in 1972 had seen their mortgage interest rates rise from 8% to 11% in just twelve months. By the time we got to 1976, we were paying anything from 12.25% to 14% depending on the mortgage lender. Many of us who had taken on affordable mortgages, bank loans and hire purchase agreements in the early 1970s were now financially embarrassed and struggling to pay the bills. Some had also been tempted to spend heavily on their newly acquired Barclaycard and Access credit cards, which made matters even worse. Fortunately, credit cards were still fairly new to us and not yet widely used in the UK (Barclaycard was the UK's first credit card, launched in 1967, and Access was the second, launched in 1972). Those of us who were raising young families at the time soon discovered that children of the 1970s were not as understanding or as easily satisfied as we had been in our 1950s childhood.

Unlike back then, there was now tremendous peer pressure on children to have all the latest clothes and playthings. They were influenced by television images like never before. Gone were the days of kids settling for a new skipping rope or a cricket bat; we were now in the realms of Raleigh Chopper bikes and Stereobelts (the first portable, personal stereo audio cassette players, pre-dating the Sony Walkman of 1979–80). It was a sharp lesson in the reality of how much things had changed since the war. Despite having to make cutbacks in our spending during these uncertain times, we were still happily overindulging our children, lavishing expensive gifts on them that we could never have even dreamed of when we were kids. We were spoiling them, and year on year we were increasing their expectations as to the number and value of the items that they could demand for their birthday and Christmas presents, not to mention all the pocket money and other treats we heaped upon them. We were only practicing the generosity we had known during the hard times of the 1950s and the happy-go-lucky 1960s, but many of us baby boomers overdid it. Although our children enjoyed the benefits of our love and generosity at the time, they and future generations of young parents will have to suffer the effects of an ever-increasing leaning towards materialism and a lack of respect for the value of money. We were cultivating a something-for-nothing attitude in the young and we would suffer for our actions in future years. We set these wheels in motion in the 1970s and children's expectations continued to grow throughout the 1980s and 1990s, and on into the third millennium. By the year 2012, our children's children might well be casually asking granny to buy them a £400–£500 Apple iPad for Christmas, and it is hard to see how this spiralling trend will ever be curbed. It's a long way from the spinning tops we played with in the 1950s.

The 1970s was a fantastic time to be young and anyone who grew up in this decade will tell you what a colourful, exciting and fun time it was. Most have fond memories of their childhood and teenage years and feel they were fortunate to have grown up in that era. To the rest of the 1970s population, the period is probably best remembered as being one of extreme trouble and strife. Colourful, yes, but more importantly it was a problematical decade for all but the young and carefree. The mood of the country seemed to be light years away from the heady days of the Swinging Sixties. All around us there was evidence that the nation was in turmoil. The peaceful, post-war country we had known since birth changed on 12 January 1971 when terrorists representing the Angry Brigade began a bombing campaign. Targeting banks and embassies in Britain, as well as government ministers' homes, they even attacked a BBC outside-broadcasting vehicle that was covering the Miss World competition. These were the first bombings we baby boomers had ever experienced and the first the country had seen since the Second World War. In response, London's Metropolitan Police Service immediately established The Bomb Squad at their Scotland Yard headquarters in London. In October that same year an IRA terrorist group planted a bomb in the men's toilet at the Top of the Tower rotating restaurant, which was situated on the thirty-fourth floor of the Post Office Tower in central London. Fortunately, no one was injured but the building suffered extensive damage. The restaurant did reopen for business but was eventually shut down in 1980 because of on-going security fears. Everyone was shocked by that 1971 incident and it was to change our lives forever. From that moment, we all began to realise that the peace and safety we had known and enjoyed for the previous twenty-six years had come to an end and life in Britain would never be the same again. These were the darkest days of the Northern Ireland conflict and throughout the 1970s various factions of the IRA continued to carry out indiscriminate bombings and assassinations, and many innocent people were killed and injured. Other terrorist groups representing various causes and beliefs were also active during the 1970s, and the combined effect was frightening. The worst atrocity during the 1970s was the Birmingham pub bombings on 21 November 1974, when twenty-one were killed and 182 suffered injuries. It is still not know who carried out the Birmingham pub bombings; the IRA denied responsibility.

These terrorist activities left us shaken and insecure and they added chaos and fear to our country's already turbulent problems; our everyday lives were becoming increasingly stressful and difficult because of unrest whilst at work. The workplace had become an unstable pressure pot that regularly erupted. There was definitely a much more confrontational attitude than there had been in the 1960s. We were now witnessing constant battles of will between management and workers; there was a clear 'them and us' approach to everything and, all at once, there was an abundance of militant shop stewards and union leaders shouting from the rooftops and ready to call their members out on strike on a whim. The unions made it impossible for businesses to implement any new ideas they might have had to increase productivity, and they fought tooth and nail to stop any form of rationalisation. More employers than ever were falling victim to the 'closed shop', which meant that a worker could not be employed in certain jobs unless he or she was a member of the relevant union. The practice of 'demarcation', when one category of worker was not allowed to do the work of another, became intolerable and soon hundreds of 'how many men does it take to…?' jokes were doing the rounds. Shop stewards were unrealistic in their demands and totally inflexible when interpreting the rules of demarcation, and they seemed to delight in the power they had to bring businesses to a halt. The idea of protecting skilled jobs seemed quite reasonable in practical situations (for example, not letting a cleaner change a light bulb when there was an electrician on site), but the lines of demarcation became ridiculous and there were silly situations arising, like a factory worker being unable to move a small box out of the way and an office worker unable to shift a desk a few inches. The slightest infringement of the rules could lead to a walkout (instant strike action). The unions were tougher than ever, professing that they would to do anything to uphold the rights of the downtrodden workers and protect their jobs. Many people still had to work in unsafe conditions and many more had stories of being exploited by their employers, and so it seemed sensible for workers to back the stance that the unions were taking. The unions, however, made one demand after another: more pay, fewer hours, extra holidays and better conditions. The demands were endless and it was just a matter of what action they had to take to get what they wanted.

Arthur Scargill, then leader of the Yorkshire region of the National Union of Mineworkers, said, 'You get as much as you are prepared to go out and take.' The unions were prepared to call strike after strike to bring the employers to their knees, but they were also bringing the country to its knees and putting their workers' jobs in jeopardy. The 1973 industrial action by the coal miners coincided with the OAPEC oil embargo and subsequent oil price rise. The combined effect was to cause a British energy crisis over the winter of 1973–74. The energy crisis led to the prime minister, Edward Heath, limiting the use of electricity in most commercial and industrial premises to three specific days each week from 31 December 1973. This became known as the 'three-day week': a period of short pay, power cuts and television closing down at 10.30 p.m. every night. Petrol ration books were also issued in anticipation of the government having to ration the amount of petrol motorists could use and Ted Heath asked the British people to heat only one room in their houses over the winter to save energy. The prime minister and his Cabinet had seriously considered banning people from heating more than one room in their homes as part of an emergency energy-saving package, but an all-out ban never happened. Other restrictions that the government had secretly planned but never implemented included a compulsory 50mph speed limit, banning Sunday motoring, shortening the school week to four days and banning Christmas package tours abroad. They also drew up a list of one hundred mains-operated domestic appliances that they proposed should be either taxed or withdrawn from used during the emergency and possibly after. These included such things as electric food mixers, heated hostess trolleys, electric toothbrushes, coffee percolators and desk fans, as well as labour-saving equipment such as electric hedge trimmers.

The 1970s was an awful period of unrest with strike after strike, resulting in the average number of working days lost each year through industrial disputes being 12.9 million, compared to 7.2 million in the 1980s, 660,000 in the 1990s and 692,000 in the 2000s. The number of working days lost in the 1970s peaked at 29.4 million during the so-called 'winter of discontent' in 1979. There were 4,500 disputes in the 1978–79 period alone. Managers spent most of their time negotiating with the unions instead of running their businesses and for some time it did seem like the lunatics were running the asylum. The unions appeared to be in control and were not afraid to wield their newfound power. Unfortunately, some union leaders seemed to lose sight of their main objectives and appeared more interested in breaking businesses rather than protecting members' jobs and increasing benefits for them. Some militant union leaders showed no sympathy or understanding of a company's need to maintain profitability in order to stay in business and provide jobs. There was no mercy, and any sign of weakness in management resulted in a further tightening of the screw. Union-organised marches were a common sight in every town and city throughout the UK. Many 'closed-shop' businesses were known to be over staffed but employers were unable to do anything about it for fear of strike action. With so much over staffing, absenteeism was rife. The wartime spirit of everyone pulling together for the good of the country was nowhere to be seen, and skiving and poor workmanship became general topics of conversation. There was talk that night workers in the print industry, which was mainly based in London's Fleet Street at the time, were regularly sleeping through their shifts. Disgruntled workers in the motor industry lacked the motivation to produce good-quality goods. The sense of pride in workmanship wore thin through the week and by the time Friday arrived it had manifested itself into a less-than-caring attitude and an increase in absenteeism. In fact, a brand-new car that was found to be faulty was often referred to as a 'Friday car'; the inference being that it was made on a Friday when nobody much cared. Our entire daily lives seemed to be consumed with matters concerning industrial action, even if we were non-union and not directly involved at all in any kind of dispute.

Union leaders were high profile and famous. Ordinary people in the street who struggled to remember the names of leading politicians of the day found it easy to recite union leaders' names and industrial action was regularly used as a theme for television sitcoms and comedy shows. There were, however, certainly workplace issues that needed addressing during the 1970s. Some things had not advanced very much since the war, especially sex discrimination in the workplace. Considering that the majority of women were in some kind of employment, there were still very few women managers because men were usually promoted ahead of them. Despite the Equal Pay Act of 1970, it was also still common practice for women to be paid less than men for doing the same job and there were still a number of jobs that were, in a derogatory way, considered to be women's jobs. It was hard for women to be taken seriously at work when glamour calendars and pin-up pictures of topless women were still displayed on office and factory walls throughout the land. Yes, there were a great many issues for union leaders to get their teeth into – not least greater equality for women and sex discrimination in general, racial discrimination and matters of health and safety – but they seemed to be consumed with wage and benefit demands that were crippling the country.

Ultimately, whatever the unions achieved for their members came at a high cost to us all, with high inflation, high taxes, spending cuts, public money ploughed into troubled industries, businesses closing down and rising unemployment. Industrial unrest was worse than it had been since the British General Strike of 1926. In the period from 1965 to 1980, 2 million manufacturing jobs were lost and by the end of the 1970s, many workers were getting fed up with all the strikes. More and more were rejecting strike action and crossing the picket lines to get on with their work. They began to see that change was inevitable; British industry had to modernise to compete in world markets. Like it or not, we had to make way for new ideas and find better ways of running our industries. There was a need to organise workforces to work in different and more effective ways and this would mean that some of the old jobs would have to go. Jobs for life were becoming a thing of the past.

From 1970 to 1974 we had a Conservative government, and in 1973 the then Prime Minister, Edward Heath, took the United Kingdom into the European Economic Community (Common Market). We then had a Labour government from 1974 to 1979, and in accordance with their general election manifesto of October 1974, they allowed the British people to have a referendum on whether or not Britain should stay in the Common Market on renegotiated terms or leave it entirely. The Labour government recommended a 'Yes' vote, even though it later emerged that seven out of the twenty-three Cabinet members wanted us to withdraw. The Conservative Party, under the leaderships of Edward Heath (1970–75) and Margaret Thatcher (1975–90), also campaigned for a 'Yes' vote. Just over 67% of the British voting public believed all the rhetoric and supported the 'Yes' campaign to stay in the EEC. After all, surely it would be good for us to be part of the Common Market – we were told that it was just a way for us to improve trading with other members of the European Community; just think of all those British manufacturing jobs it would create; there was no possibility that it could ever lead to the erosion of our national sovereignty and a transferral of powers to Europe. It was just what it said on the tin – a Common Market, that's all. And 67% of us fell for it.

For many of us baby boomers, the negative events of the 1970s will score highly on our list of lifetime memories, albeit ones that we would perhaps rather forget. These may well have been days of trouble and strife and the darkest days of the Northern Ireland conflict, but it would be wrong to paint a picture of complete misery throughout the UK. There was indeed a lot of good stuff packed into those ten years, and many of us have very fond, personal memories of happy times and events that touched our lives back then. The 1970s weren't just about power cuts and the dead being left unburied. Okay, so it was the decade in which the dumbing down of educational standards first began in England and Wales, when the Labour government abolished grammar schools for virtually all but the wealthy, softened all forms of discipline in schools and removed spelling and handwriting from the marking criteria, but perhaps they were right; with all of the electronic communications and abbreviated text messaging of today, does anyone really need to be able to spell or write legibly?

Very often, silly and unimportant things crop up in our daily lives to stir light-hearted memories of days gone by, and we are reminded of so many things through radio and television and in books and newspapers. Simple things transport us straight back to the 1970s, like the old Polaroid instant cameras that we all wanted to get our hands on back then, the sounds of Demis Roussos' songs on the radio, K-tel records and the products they regularly promoted in their television adverts, such as the K-tel Brush-O-Matic. Our way of life has altered so much since then. Unfussy pleasures, like going down the local pub, have been diminished because our changing British lifestyle and new laws have forced many of the local pubs that were once packed full of regulars to close down. In the 1970s, it was still common practice for workers to go to the pub at lunchtime to enjoy a liquid lunch. This was before many of the big old pubs were turned into gastropubs to attract families with young children. It was a time when a pub was still a sanctuary for adults, one of the few places in which adults could take refuge from the delightful sounds and activities of their darling little children. It was a time when you had to search hard to find a pub that sold food any more substantial than a cheese roll. A local pub was a place in which old boys played dominoes at a table in the corner while the true athletes played darts and drank pints of Watney's Red Barrel and other keg beers. Women's favourite drinks included port and lemon, vodka and orange, lager and lime, and perhaps a Babycham at Christmas. And, of course, everyone's favourite cocktail drink at Christmas was the Snowball, a mixture of Advocaat and lemonade. If you were very grand you would serve it with a glacé cherry on top. If you lived in a very posh house then you might well have had one of those luxuriously padded, bow-fronted cocktail cabinets fitted into the corner of your front room with your very own spirit-dispensing optics attached to the back wall – very tasteful.

People crowd on top of a van during VE Day celebrations in London on 8 May 1945. (*Getty Images*)

A 1949 recruitment advert for women to join the newly formed Women's Royal Army Corps. Women had to be between 18 and 30 years old. The job offered a smart uniform, comfortable quarters, thirty days' leave with pay and the opportunity to travel and see new romantic places.

Local children gather to celebrate VE Day on 8 May 1945.

1949 – Typical scene of office life as it was in the late 1940s through to the early 1960s. The style of typewriters would have modernised over time but little else.

1949 – Mother and daughter pose for a picture in their small front garden in a back street in Battersea, London. Battersea Power Station is featured in the background.

Post-war baby boomer children being cared for by nurses in the children's ward of a hospital in 1952.

A group of children playing a game of soldiers (*Picture Post*, 'The Yanks in England', 1952). (*Getty Images*)

A small boy poses for his picture in a traffic-free side street in central London in 1952.

A baby in a pram enjoys the fresh air outside a house in central London in 1953.

5 Feb 1953 – A crowd of children rush to get into a sweetshop as it opens its doors on the day that sweet rationing ended. (*Getty Images*)

Children's street party held on 2 June 1953 in south London to celebrate the coronation of Queen Elizabeth II.

A family dressed up in their Sunday best to pose for a photograph outside a house in Sussex in 1955.

Three children pose for a photograph on their way to a street party in central London to celebrate the coronation of Queen Elizabeth II on 2 June 1953.

Three young women play records on a Dansette-style portable record player in their living room in the late 1950s.

Left: A young couple jiving at a firm's staff dance in the City of London in 1960.

Below left: Two young boys enjoy a day out in Trafalgar Square, London in the early 1960s. School uniform was often used as best clothes when going somewhere special.

Below right: Teenage boys dressed up for a night out in the early 1960s. The 1950s fashions were still evident at the time with Slim Jim ties, winkle-picker shoes, trousers with turn-ups and hair that was styled into a Brylcreemed 'quiff'.

A typical high-street scene with no parking restrictions from the early 1960s in Oakham.

Mid-1960s – A large group of commuters on the steps of the platforms at Fenchurch Street Station, London. (*John Gay/ English Heritage. NMR/Mary Evans*)

Above: Late 1960s – A young hippy couple (the man having the obligatory 'Love' painted on his face and both with flowers in their hair) being gawped at by mods and the older generation alike. (© *Mary Evans Picture Library/BILL COWARD*)

Above right: 1975 – Fans of The Osmonds, some of whom have waited all night, cheer the group as they arrive at Capital Radio's offices in London. (*Getty Images*)

Right: In the 1970s, collecting Green Shield Stamps was very popular. Shops and garages gave them out to reward loyal shoppers. Books of stamps could be exchanged for goods at one of the Green Shield Stamps catalogue shops around the country.

Above: A 1970s office worker surrounded by paperwork, ledgers and rubber ink stamps, using pen and paper, with no sign at all of a computer or other electronic gadgets.

Opposite top: A vintage car chauffeured by a 1970s-style driver in flares and long hair.

Opposite bottom: 1977 – Parents gather round as children take part in a space-hopper race during a street party in Essex, in honour of the Silver Jubilee of Queen Elizabeth II. (© *Mary Evans / The Watts Collection*)

Huge crowds gathered to witness and celebrate the wedding of Prince Charles to Lady Diana Spencer on 29 July 1981. (© *Illustrated London News Ltd/Mary Evans*)

Early 1980s style with the latest, must-have, brick-size mobile phone.

Diana, Princess of Wales
in the 1980s.

Prime Minister, Margaret
Thatcher in the 1980s.

5 Sept 1997 – The Prince of Wales, Prince William and Prince Harry look at floral tributes to Diana, Princess of Wales outside Kensington Palace. (*Getty Images*)

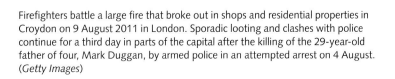

Firefighters battle a large fire that broke out in shops and residential properties in Croydon on 9 August 2011 in London. Sporadic looting and clashes with police continue for a third day in parts of the capital after the killing of the 29-year-old father of four, Mark Duggan, by armed police in an attempted arrest on 4 August. (*Getty Images*)

It was in the 1970s, after having spent several years since leaving school slumbering in armchairs, that we suddenly decided we wanted to get fit. Following a keep-fit trend in America, we British began joining newly opened gyms, playing squash and even going out jogging in the street, in public! This was a new and unusual sight on our streets back then and the pioneers of British jogging were very brave, attracting strange looks wherever they went. At the same time, we were all trying desperately to give up smoking after being shown horrible pictures of damaged human lungs on our television screens. A growing group of environmentalists were also hell bent on making us feel guilty about the damage we were doing to our environment and we were becoming more conscious of the world around us. The government was interfering more and more in matters relating to the state of our health and the way we lived our lives. For the first time, cholesterol and blood pressure became part of the ordinary person's vocabulary. When we weren't jogging to keep fit, we occupied our spare time making homemade wine and beer, another fad of the seventies, as was renting all those poor-quality VHS films from the high street video shops. However, our newfound fitness regime was subjected to competition from increasing amounts of takeaway fish-and-chip suppers, McDonald's burgers and all of the Kentucky Fried Chicken that we ate to stifle the hunger pangs brought on after we gave up smoking.

We baby boomers were a bit disgruntled in 1971 when the United Kingdom changed to the decimal system for currency. Employers had to organise training sessions to teach their employees how to calculate the new currency and handle the new coins. Ironically, the specially formed Decimal Currency Board filmed a promotional video for the new decimal currency, featuring its chairman, Lord Fiske, at a Woolworths store in London. Woolworths was thought to typify the British high street because most people regularly shopped at their local Woolworths store. Who would ever have thought that the day would come when they would completely disappear from the high street, as they did over a two-week period following Christmas 2008 (807 stores closed and 27,000 job losses following a period in administration) – no more Woolies' pick 'n' mix sweets.

We witnessed a lot of landmark events in the 1970s and there are many for us to be proud of: these include the ending of the Vietnam War in 1975, the first turbojet-powered supersonic passenger airliner Concorde coming into service (retired from service in 2003), the street parties of 1977 to mark the Queen's Silver Jubilee, Margaret Thatcher becoming our first female prime minister in 1979, teenagers of 18 and over being able to vote in a UK election for the first time (the voting age was reduced from 21 to 18 in 1969), the first pocket calculators and home video game consoles going on sale (remember that primitive tennis game we played through our television sets), the first domestic microwave ovens and video cassette recorders appearing in UK shops, the arrivals of the Raleigh Chopper bicycles and the Sony Walkman personal stereos, and it was also the decade in which colour television broadcasting became the norm in British homes.

The 1970s has certainly had its fair share of bad press over the years, and it is true that the decade is somewhat overshadowed by the excitement surrounding the 1960s and the glamorous Sloane Ranger lifestyle and yuppie dynamism of the 1980s, but we learned much and gained plenty from the 1970s and anyone who has trouble remembering anything good about the decade should start by reflecting on the long hot summer of 1976. Happy days!

30-somethings in Leg Warmers

A deep recession, crippling inflation, high unemployment, strikes and widespread rioting marred events of the 1980s. The National Health Service was also failing as more and more health authorities across the country were going into the red and, despite higher spending levels and increases in staff numbers, waiting lists were growing longer and hospital wards were being closed to patients. Britain fought a war in the far-distant Falkland Islands while at home we endured the continuing threat of terrorism. We were just four months into the new decade when a six-man terrorist team seized control of the Iranian Embassy building in South Kensington, London and took twenty-six people hostage. This came to be known as the Iranian Embassy Siege and it lasted from 30 April to

5 May 1980. We watched the television news coverage as events unfolded over the six days and on the final day the terrorists killed one of the hostages and threw his body out of the embassy. This prompted the British Special Air Services (SAS) to make an assault on the building. Having abseiled from the roof, a team of SAS soldiers broke in through the embassy windows and killed five of the six terrorists. The entire SAS operation took just seventeen minutes. The sixth terrorist was captured and went on to serve a twenty-seven-year prison sentence. As in the 1970s, the IRA were at the forefront of terrorist bombing activities in mainland Britain and three years after they killed Airey Neave with a car bomb as he drove out of the Palace of Westminster car park, they returned to London to cause more carnage. On 20 July 1982, they carried out two bombings. The first of these targeted members of the Household Cavalry in Hyde Park and two hours later they bombed the bandstand in Regent's Park, killing members of the Royal Green Jackets. In all, the IRA killed eleven soldiers and injured fifty people including civilians on that ill-fated summer's day.

Earlier that year, we found ourselves immersed in a conflict with Argentina over the sovereignty of the Falkland Islands and its surroundings. This followed the invasion and occupation of the Falkland Islands and South Georgia by Argentine forces on Friday 2 April 1982. Neither side officially declared war but Prime Minister Margaret Thatcher immediately responded to the invasion of the British-dependent territory by sending a taskforce of 127 ships and a nuclear-powered submarine to take back the islands. At the time, the Falkland Islands were a place on the other side of the world that many of us knew little or nothing about. It was 8,000 miles from mainland Britain with a land area about the same size as Yorkshire and a population of around 3,140, similar to that of a small village in middle England. The conflict lasted seventy-four days and a total of 255 British servicemen and three female Falkland Island civilians were killed. The Argentine losses were considerably larger with 649 killed, including sixteen civilian sailors. The successful recapture of the Falkland Islands from Argentina showed we had strong leadership and this helped to increase Thatcher and her government's popularity with the British public.

Meanwhile, back at home we remained in fear of imminent terrorist attacks and we did not have to wait long for the next major attack to happen. On the 17 December 1983, the IRA planted a car bomb outside the side entrance of Harrods on Hans Crescent in Knightsbridge. The bomb exploded killing six people and leaving ninety injured on one of the busiest shopping days of the year. For those of us who were not directly touched by any of the terrorists' bombings during the eighties, the one that probably remains most firmly in our minds is the bombing of the Grand Hotel, Brighton on 12 October 1984 when the IRA attempted to assassinate Margaret Thatcher and members of her Cabinet who were attending the Conservative Party conference there. Five people were killed and 34 were injured, including some who were left permanently disabled. The final IRA bombing of the 1980s happened on the 22 September 1989 at the Royal Marines' barracks in Deal, Kent when eleven marines were killed and twenty-one were left injured. The horrible carnage and destruction caused by these and all of the other terrorist atrocities carried out by the IRA during their campaigns of mass murder left permanent stains in our minds, but the most appalling single terrorist action of the 1980s was not carried out by the IRA. This atrocity was the work of an entirely different terrorist group, thought to be of Libyan origin. On 21 December 1988, Pan Am Flight 103 was blown up over Lockerbie in Scotland, killing all 243 passengers and sixteen crew members. Eleven people in the town of Lockerbie were also killed when they were hit by pieces of wreckage falling to the ground. Several terrorist groups claimed responsibility for the bombing but it was alleged to be the work of Libyan terrorists and on 31 January 2001 Abdelbaset al-Megrahi, the head of security for Libyan Arab Airlines and alleged Libyan intelligence officer, was convicted of murder by a panel of three Scottish judges and sentenced to life imprisonment. This was a really scary time in our lives; we were constantly reminded of the threat from all sorts of terrorist assassins and crackpot killers.

In 1981, US President Ronald Reagan was shot in the chest outside a hotel in Washington DC, and in the same year Pope John Paul II was shot in St Peter's Square, Vatican City; both were seriously injured and nearly died. Inspired by the murder of John Lennon in December 1980 and these two high-profile assassination attempts in the spring of 1981, in June that year a 17-year-old unemployed youth from Folkestone in Kent fired six blank shots at the Queen as she rode her horse down the mall during a Trooping the Colour ceremony. Fortunately, the Queen managed to bring her horse under control and she escaped unharmed. The youth said that he did it to become famous: 'I will become the most famous teenager in the world.' I won't fuel his ambitions by naming him but he went on to serve three years of a five-year sentence and was soon forgotten. There are a lot of crazy people in the world but they seemed to be especially active in the 1980s.

The decade was far from being all doom and gloom but there was an awful lot going on and once again we had to cope with a great many changes affecting all aspects of life. It was a very exciting period but for many it was also a nerve-racking time. Memories of events surrounding the untimely death of John Lennon on 8 December 1980 take our minds straight back to the start of the decade and act as an aide-memoire to what was going on in our lives around that time. John Lennon and The Beatles had been a major part of our adolescent lives and his shocking murder was a wake-up call to remind us of how dangerous a place the world can be for innocent people going about their everyday lives. His death was also a milestone in our own personal lives because we now knew without doubt that The Beatles could never get back together again.

Most of us were touched by the early 1980s recession, high inflation, high taxes, redundancies and high unemployment. Some fared better than others, but we all suffered in one way or another. We had seen unemployment rise steadily in the early to mid-1970s and then surge in numbers during the late 1970s and early 1980s. There were 1 million people unemployed in Britain in 1972 when the population was

56 million. By 1982, the population had risen to 56.5 million and the number of people unemployed had shot up to an astonishing figure of 3.07 million, the highest number since the 1930s. One in eight people of working age were now unemployed, 12.5% of the workforce. Northern Ireland was worst hit with unemployment reaching almost 20%. Scotland and most parts of England experienced 15% unemployment, while the south-east fared better with levels of around 10%. More than 750,000 people were now classed as long-term unemployed. The then Labour Party leader, Michael Foot, said that whereas in 1979 there were five people chasing each job, there were now thirty-two people chasing every vacancy, and in some parts of the country the figure was double that. Unemployment levels in Britain were almost the highest in Europe, only second to Belgium. The levels of increase were mainly due to businesses closing down and British industry being forced to sharpen up its act and restructure organisations to survive the economic recession. The heavy industries, like car manufacturing, mining, shipbuilding and steel, were the hardest hit. Unlike previous governments, the Thatcher government was not prepared to bail out these industries every time they got themselves into trouble. Despite strike action, significant job losses were now inevitable across all of these industries. This was a great shock to those who had buried their heads in the sand throughout the industrial strife of 1970s and refused to accept that the long-standing 'jobs for life' culture had to end. Traditional manufacturing industries such as British Leyland had to shut factories and

make large-scale redundancies, and many well-known brand names like Biba, Laker Airways and Triumph Motorcycles went out of business. Any kind of work was hard to come by and many industrial workers found that the skills they had acquired over a number of years were no longer in demand. For many, their only chance of finding work was to retrain and possibly move to another part of the country. Some tradesmen had to find work in other European countries, often living in dingy digs or worksite cabins, sometimes having to share a bed with another shift worker, one on days and the other on nights – the practice was called 'hotbedding'.

With so many men being put out of work and traditional jobs becoming harder to find, more and more families were turning to the woman of the house to become the main breadwinner. During the period from 1980 to 1985, more than 1 million women joined the workforce. Whether the men could have done any of these jobs is questionable because different types of jobs were now being created. The country was moving away from manufacturing and instead developing service industries. There was a large-scale movement of jobs away from cities and into outlying areas where new business parks were being built. This was often done by firms looking to revitalise themselves while making the most of new technology and cutting costs. We were producing fewer British goods and importing more foreign-made products. Employers were looking for people with good presentation skills and brainpower to fill the new jobs in banking, retailing and telemarketing. There was also an increase in professional recruitment jobs and in market research companies. Often, women were found to be better suited to these types of jobs, especially jobs that required direct communication with customers. In the main, women were still being paid less than men for doing the same job but these newly created jobs gave women the opportunity to close the gap and in some cases they were paid the same as there was a fixed pay scale for the job. Women were at last getting into occupations that would provide them with long-term careers. These new jobs enabled them to gain the knowledge and experience they needed to qualify for promotion into managerial positions. Women with ambition were now beginning to be taken seriously in the workplace.

An ever-increasing number of businesses were also using what were called mainframe computers to maintain records and process work. These machines were still very large and they needed to be housed in special environmentally controlled rooms and managed by trained computer operators. Computer workstations began to appear on individual desks during the 1980s but most of these were only capable of drawing down information from the central mainframe computer. The information was transferred onto the mainframe by staff trained in data processing. At this time, many firms were also still using the old-style, punch-card system, which involved specially trained keypunch operators, invariably women, inputting information onto small thin cards using card-punch machines. Big firms had huge rooms specially designed to accommodate large numbers of card-punch machines. In the 1960s, 1970s and 1980s, key punch operating jobs were plentiful and they were considered to be good and secure.

Despite the widespread use of business computers and the increasing amount of modern office equipment like the fax machine, large numbers of people were still employed for clerical work and open-plan offices filled with typists and accounts clerks were still the norm for much of the 1980s. As we moved through the decade, however, more and more typists and punch operators were ditching their old IBM Golfball typewriters and card-punch machines to retrain as word processor operators, and more and more office correspondence was being dealt with by these word processors. In 1986 we saw the first Microsoft Windows operating system being used in Britain. This was considered a marvel at the time but it was slow to catch on here. The introduction of word processors into offices was a major problem for women returning to work after a career break to bring up a family or whatever, because they were not familiar with modern office equipment and procedures. Many had left office work a few years earlier when manual typewriters and clipboards were still the norm. Although a great number of these job seekers were still only in their 20s and 30s, in the modern-day office of the late 1980s they were regarded as dinosaurs and a lot of them found it very difficult to get back into office work. Many had to sign-up for night school courses to get retrained at their own expense.

The stereotypical workplace image of yesteryear when women were cast as typists, Girl Fridays and tea ladies was slowly disappearing and we were seeing increasing numbers of female bosses sitting behind the executive desks. We were becoming used to seeing women in powerful positions and more and more workers were having to adjust to working for a woman for the first time, something that the older generations in the 1980s must have found difficult after years of male dominance at their place of work. Some workers did have difficulty adjusting to women giving the orders, and this was not just the male workers. Some women struggled to adapt and confrontations were not uncommon, with accusations of women bosses being tougher and more demanding than their male counterparts. Perhaps there was some truth in the old adage that women had to be tough to succeed in business.

Whether by choice or otherwise, some baby boomers started their own families in the mid-1960s when they were still teenagers. In the early 1980s, many of these 1960s babies were leaving school and looking for work in the most difficult job market for fifty years. Of the 3 million unemployed, 1 million were school leavers. The poorer areas of the inner cities were particularly hit by the early 1980s recession and the spiralling levels of unemployment. In some areas there was already long-standing local unrest, sometimes due to racial tension between residents and police. In April 1981, things got out of hand and boiled over in the streets of Brixton, south London when rioting broke out and large numbers of vehicles were burned and shops damaged and looted over a three-day period. At least 364 people were injured in the riots, including 299 police officers, and eighty-two people were arrested. Following on from the Brixton riots, in July 1981 there was a ten-day period of rioting in various towns and cities around the country. Many of these riots were also sparked by local racial tensions and the disturbances were mostly in areas that had been hit hard by unemployment and recession. The worst of the riots was in Toxteth, Liverpool in which 468 police officers were injured and 500 people arrested; shops were looted, at least seventy buildings were burned out and about 100 cars were destroyed. July rioting also took place at Brixton in London, Handsworth in Birmingham, Southall in London, Hyson Green in Nottingham and Moss Side in Manchester. There were also some smaller incidences of trouble in Bedford, Bristol, Coventry, Edinburgh, Gloucester, Halifax, Leeds, Leicester, Southampton and Wolverhampton. There was a lot of racial tension and social discord but many observers believe that unemployment, boredom and imitation of events elsewhere led to much of the copycat rioting, and for some it was just an excuse to go out looting other people's property.

There were other noticeable tensions starting to fester on our streets in the 1980s as we began to observe a new and more sinister street scene developing in our major cities. We witnessed a growth in what was called the 'cardboard jungle', with a huge increase in the number of homeless people on our streets, especially in London, a large thriving capital city that was seen as a prosperous haven for discontented people from every corner of the world. Gone was the pleasure of taking an early evening stroll along the high street to do some window shopping. All of a sudden, a multi-ethnic mix of vagrants began to commandeer shop doorways for use as their sleeping quarters and the rancid smell of urine wafting up from pavements became a common airborne odour to passers-by. Shopkeepers were faced with having to wash down and disinfect their shop entrances before they could open for business each morning. Crime-related drug taking involving traditional street drugs was an ever-growing problem but there was also an increasing trend of glue sniffing among young kids. They were now sniffing all kinds of solvents including aerosols and household cleaning products, even nail varnish remover and cigarette lighter fuel. It was an extremely dangerous trend and young kids were accidentally dying through solvent abuse. We had always been used to seeing the occasional tramp or beggar walking the streets in our towns and cities, but immigrant beggars, often clutching a young child, were now accosting us in the street and there was also a new breed of home-grown professional beggar who could afford to dress in designer clothes. Some of these so-called professional beggars were said to live in the suburbs and commute into the city each day as if they were going to work. Some were even seen getting into good quality cars at the end of the day and driving themselves home. Ruthless foreign nationals were known to be using gangs of Fagin-like children to pick pockets in busy public areas. Gangs of extortionists were using a new style of threatening behaviour to extract money from motorists in the form of 'squeegee men' who would approach cars at traffic lights and smear the windscreens with dirty water then demand money from the driver. Major road junctions were littered with intimidating flower sellers weaving their way through slow-moving traffic carrying armfuls of flowers and trying to sell small bunches to anxious and gullible motorists. The British public were already fearful of possible terrorist attacks and bombings, and we were now beginning to feel threatened and unsafe going about our everyday lives, even just walking the streets.

By the turn of 1982, we were beginning to emerge from the two-year recession; inflation was coming down and was now below 10%, compared to its peak level of 22% in 1980. It continued to fall and by spring 1983 it was down to 4%, a fifteen-year low. Despite the pain of recession and the on-going high levels of unemployment, Margaret Thatcher and her Conservative government were re-elected in the 1983 UK general election. It was the most decisive general election victory any political party had enjoyed since Labour's landslide win in 1945. She was now able to confidently proceed with what was called 'Thatcherism' and implement her 'Thatcherite' policies, including the curbing of trade unions' powers and the privatisation of major utilities. British Telecom was the first in a series of big state-owned utilities to be privatised when it was floated in November 1984, with 50.2% of the shares of the new company being offered for sale to the public and BT employees. There followed a large number of floatations in the later part of the 1980s including British Gas (1986) with the 'Tell Sid' advertising campaign, British Airways (1987), British Airports Authority (1987), British Steel (1988) and the Regional Water Companies in England and Wales (1989). Such privatisations continued throughout the 1990s and beyond, and they included the Regional Electricity Companies (1990), British Coal (1994) and British Rail (1995–97).

Margaret Thatcher featured prominently in events of the 1980s as you would expect with any prime minister of any political persuasion, but Margaret Thatcher was not just any prime minister; she was our first female prime minister and she was proving to be the strongest leader we baby boomers had seen running the country in our lifetime. The British public had chosen a tough and decisive prime minister with all of the qualities needed to move the country forward from the darkest days of the 1970s, sort out our economy and get the country back on its feet. Some may question her methods and achievements but she was certainly a tough and decisive leader. People from coal-mining areas will remember her for the tough stance she took over the 1984–85 miners' strike and the subsequent closure of coalmines. Many of those who belonged to the coal-mining industry will blame her for destroying their livelihoods, breaking up communities and turning their villages into ghost towns. However, there was never going to be an easy outcome to the miners' dispute. The National Coal Board was heavily subsidised by the British taxpayer and most mines were unprofitable. Despite the subsidies, British coal was said to be costing more than coal could be bought from other countries.

Thatcher was also committed to reducing the power of the trade unions. She managed to shrink the authority of the militant union bosses with tough new laws requiring pre-strike ballots and an end to 'closed shop' policies, and the unions would now also be held responsible for any illegal strikes. She introduced measures to bring down the high cost of state welfare and control benefit abuse by tightening the rules for welfare state benefit and carrying out more means testing. Her priority had been to get inflation down and she expected private employers to create the majority of jobs. She encouraged people to stand on their own two feet and not expect the state to be a universal provider.

Before becoming prime minister, Thatcher was known to the general public as 'Thatcher, Thatcher, Milk Snatcher': the woman who did away with free school milk in 1970 when she was secretary of state for education in Edward Heath's government of the time. As prime minister in the 1980s, she made more fundamental changes affecting children's education, including replacing GCE O levels and CSE exams with new GCSE examinations, and abolishing all forms of corporal punishment in state schools. Some might say these changes added to the damage already done by the Labour government when they began dumbing-down education and discipline standards in schools during the 1970s. The combined effects of these policies would lead to serious repercussions in years to come when education and discipline standards would be seen to be broken and it would be recognised that we needed to go back to basics. Possibly the most controversial thing Thatcher did while in government was introduce the short-lived Poll Tax in 1989; more formally known as the Community Charge, it replaced the traditional local authority rates system with a single flat-rate tax for every adult. Huge numbers of people either refused or couldn't afford to pay the new Poll Tax, which made the tax impossible to police because of insufficient numbers of police, bailiffs, courts and prison cells. The feeling against the new tax was so strong that its introduction led to Poll Tax riots in towns and cities across the country, especially in Central London. The nationwide fury and condemnation of the Poll Tax, especially in the north of England and in Scotland, contributed to the downfall of Margaret Thatcher the following year. Even her most loyal supporters thought she was showing signs of grandeur exceeding her position when following the birth of her first grandchild in March 1989 she announced, 'We have become a grandmother.'

Thatcher may not have always got things right but she was clear-thinking and not afraid to make difficult decisions, even if it made her unpopular. Whether at home or abroad, no one messed with Margaret Thatcher, and it was widely reported that she only needed four hours sleep a night. Amazing! She had so much energy and an eternally optimistic 'go for it' approach to life. She wanted people to take more responsibility and strive to improve their lives, whatever their background or circumstances. She encouraged home ownership and made it possible for council tenants to buy their council house or flat at a discounted value depending on how long they had been a rent-paying council tenant. This 'Right to Buy' scheme came into being with the Housing Act of 1980 and opened the floodgates for hundreds of thousands of tenants to buy the council home in which they lived. More than a million council properties were sold in this way during the 1980s alone. Thatcher also encouraged more people to start their own businesses. Her rhetoric gave the impression that anyone could be an entrepreneur, even those who had no experience at all in risk taking, and we were all tempted to have a go. Many were attracted to the idea of going it alone after being made redundant, and by 1984 nearly 2.5 million of us were running our own businesses, almost a million more than a decade before. The Thatcher government also introduced several new schemes to stop the unemployed becoming long-term dole claimants. These included a Youth Training Scheme (YTS) to get young people suitably trained for work, and several other schemes to help other unemployed people find suitable work again. They also started the Enterprise Zone scheme for job-creating employers and the Enterprise Allowance Scheme, which guaranteed an income of £40 per week to any unemployed person who set up their own business, but these would-be entrepreneurs had to produce a proper business plan and have at least £1,000 of their own money to fund the start up (bearing in mind that according to the Office of National Statistics, in 1983 the average annual wage in the UK was £7,700).

When we baby boomers were looking for our very first jobs back in the 1960s, the mood was fresh and optimistic and many of us were keen to seek out new and better job opportunities than those that had been available to our parents when they were starting out. In many cases we were better educated than our parents and grandparents and we had the extra advantage of knowledge gained through television while we were growing up, unlike our parents. To us, the world seemed a much smaller and less-daunting place than it may have been to generations before. In many cases, we were more worldly wise and adventurous, and some of us became the first in our family to move away from the local area in which we grew up. A lot of us were not content to follow the traditional paths our parents and grandparents had taken, working down the mines, in steel production or in shipbuilding, for example. We were less willing to clock in at the same factory gates and do the same routine work for the rest of our lives. We could see other job and career opportunities opening up in new and developing areas of business and industry, and we had the confidence to seek them out. The trend of travelling distances to work and willingness to move home for a job grew in the 1970s and by the time the 1980s job crisis arrived we were well used to the possibility of having to commute long distances to work. By now, most of us had also acquired a new job-seeking qualification that was somewhat absent during the 1970s – flexibility.

The economic recovery did eventually come, but it took a few years. Unemployment stayed above 3 million until the spring of 1987 and then it began to fall dramatically. People living in the Midlands and the south of England definitely needed some good news after being hit by the worst storm to batter England in 284 years. The hurricane-force storm killed at least twenty-two people and caused widespread devastation, mostly in the south-east of England where gusts of 120mph were recorded. By spring 1988 unemployment was down below 2.5 million and by the end of 1989 the figure was just above 1.6 million. The economic measures taken by Thatcher's government, which included financial dereg- ulation and the 1986 tax reforms, led to an economic boom, often called the Lawson Boom (Nigel Lawson was chancellor of the exchequer from 1983–89). Indeed, from 1983 to 1988, those of us who were fortunate enough to have a job benefited from a sizeable reduction in the basic rate of income tax, which went down from 30% to 25%, and the highest earners celebrated a reduction in the top rate from 60% to 40%, but the Lawson boom led to inflation rising from 3.4% to 8% and interest rates almost doubling in the late-1980s. To make matters worse, by the end of the 1980s the housing market was on the verge of collapse. Data collected by Nationwide, one of the UK's biggest mortgage providers, shows that in 1980 the average cost of a house in the UK was £22,677 (equivalent to the sum of about £78,000 in 2011) and apart from a small fall towards the end of 1981, prices rose steadily throughout the 1980s until the last few months of December 1989 when prices went into free-fall. In the autumn of 1989, average house prices were £62,782 (equivalent to the sum of about £117,000 in 2011); by December they had dropped to £61,495 and by March 1990 they were down to £59,587.

Love her of hate her, Margaret Thatcher still arouses the same extreme emotions today as she did when she was at the height of her power back in the 1980s. Whether you see her as a heroine or a villain is a matter of opinion and that usually depends on one's own personal experiences. Whatever your point of view, when our thoughts turn to the 1980s we can't help but remember her: the Iron Lady of politics. She was undeniably one of the two leading ladies of the decade. The other was Diana, Princess of Wales, the fresh-faced and naive young beauty who captured the hearts of the nation with her elegance and charm. Images of these two influential women regularly appeared on the front pages of every national newspaper and television news and current affairs programme throughout the 1980s. They even featured in almost every 1980s episode of the satirical puppet show, *Spitting Image*. It was on 29 July 1981 that an estimated 750 million global television audience, including 28.4 million British television viewers, watched the shy 20-year-old Lady Diana Spencer marry 32-year-old heir apparent Charles, Prince of Wales at St Paul's Cathedral in London. Throughout the 1980s, Princess Diana was the most photographed woman in the world, ruthlessly pursued by paparazzi wherever she went.

As we cast our minds back to those days when we baby boomers were mere 30-somethings and the Rubik's Cube puzzle drove us completely up the wall, we also remember how addicted we were to TV shows like *Dallas* and we wonder what possessed more than 30 million viewers to dampen the joy of their Christmas by tuning in to watch the breakup of Den and Angie's marriage in *Eastenders* in 1986. This was also the decade in which we dreamed of ditching our old cine cameras for one of the new handheld camcorders, which were the size of a small suitcase at the time. Mobile phones were in their infancy and were huge, unreliable and very expensive to buy and make calls from. The early ones took hours to charge up and the charge then only lasted for a few minutes of call time. The car phone versions were much better, with a continuous source of power and proper aerials, but in addition to the high cost of the phone these cost a fortune to have professionally fitted. These early day mobile phones were all analogue with very poor signal strength. You could feel your ear warming up within seconds of starting to use one. You found yourself being constantly cut off as the signal came and went, sometimes not even managing to speak to the person at the other end before being cut off, and yet you were still charged 35p per minute and each part of a minute by the service provider for the privilege. There was no such thing as an 'all-in' deal back then and monthly mobile phone bills would run into hundreds of pounds – definitely a gadget for the wealthy. We grew accustomed to the sight of city whiz kids and celebrities sporting brick-size mobile phones with thick, rod-like aerials. These new must-have status symbols were so big that when they were being used they would almost completely bridge the gap between ones shoulder and jaw. The not-so-well-off gadget lovers continued to use 1970s-style citizen band (CB) radios to keep in touch with other like-minded CB enthusiasts when they were out and about in their cars and trucks. They used CB slang to communicate with each other with such words and phrases as, 'Got your ears on,' 'Copy,' 'Good buddy,' 'Handle,' 'Breaker 19,' 'Eyeball,' and '10-4.' The rest of us technophobes stuck to the conventional fixed-line home and office telephones for any voice-to-voice communications.

The method by which we could enjoy our own personal taste in music was also rapidly changing. The wide shoulders on the fashionable jackets we wore in the 1980s acted as a useful shelf to support and position the extraordinarily large stereo boom boxes (ghetto blasters) as close to the ear as possible. Although these were held right next to the ear, it was important for the volume and bass to be turned up as loud as possible to be sure that everyone in the whole area around us could hear every thumping beat. It seemed we had barely got used to the excitement of owning a Sony Walkman audio cassette player when compact discs were launched and at last we could listen to our favourite music without any annoying sounds of scratches and hisses. Fortunately, the record companies started re-releasing 1950s and 1960s music on CD, which was really good because we baby boomers were getting a bit too old to appreciate much of the popular music released in the 1980s by the likes of Adam and the Ants, Culture Club, Bros and Wham!. And for some of us, as much as we loved Whitney Houston's songs, we felt more of an attachment to the catalogue of music her cousin Dionne Warwick and godmother Aretha Franklin had entertained us with throughout most of our record-playing lives. Having said all of that with tongue in cheek, there was a lot of good music created during the 1980s and many songwriters and pop stars went on to develop long and successful careers, including Billy Joel, Madonna, George Michael, Kylie Minogue, Lionel Richie and Sting. And we have to admit that most of us quite liked the new romantics' style of pop music, which was epitomised by the likes of Duran Duran and Spandau Ballet. It also seemed as though Stock, Aitkin and Waterman could do no wrong with anything they produced in the way of pop music from the mid- to late 1980s. A large number of us baby boomers bought the bestselling single of the 1980s, Band Aid's, 'Do They Know It's Christmas?' We were even tempted onto the dance floor to shake our stuff to the UK's biggest-selling singles artist of the 1980s, Shakin' Stevens. Yes, much to the surprise of 1980s pop music fans, it wasn't any of the big-selling names like David Bowie, Phil Collins, Michael Jackson, Paul McCartney or Rod Stewart; it was Shakin' Stevens. He had twenty-eight top-40 hit singles in the 1980s alone, including four number ones.

As the 1980s progressed, we were beginning to see some development in television broadcasting, which gave us a much greater choice of programmes to watch and at different times of the day. In November 1982, Channel 4 began broadcasting, taking the total number of available television channels to four: BBC 1, BBC 2, ITV and Channel 4. However, these were all national terrestrial analogue channels; we were not yet blessed with multi-channel digital television. In 1983, breakfast television arrived in Britain and changed the routine of our early morning lives forever. Who could ever have imagined that we would be watching television at that time of the morning, before we went to work or took the children to school? Here in Britain, it was not yet popular practice to have a television set in the bedroom or in the kitchen, let alone have multiple television sets all around the house. Many of us had to nip in and out of the main living room to catch snippets of the topics being covered on these new early morning television breakfast shows. This was a time when television sets were enormous: as deep as they were wide and very heavy, often needing two people to lift one. Even portable television sets were huge in comparison to today's; they were large square boxes that needed to be sat upon sturdy pieces of furniture. On the plus side, we did by now have the benefit of hand-held remote controls, albeit with a limited number of functions, and these enabled us to switch back and forth between each of the breakfast television shows. Our first experience of breakfast television was on 17 January 1983 when the BBC launched their *Breakfast Time* magazine-style programme hosted by Frank Bough, Selina Scott and Nick Ross, with regular appearances from astrologer Russell Grant and fitness expert Diana Moran, better known to us as the 'Green Goddess' due to the striking colour of the leotard she wore. On 1 February 1983, just two weeks after the first BBC *Breakfast Time* went on air, ITV launched its own flagship *TV-am* breakfast-time programmes, *Daybreak* and *Good Morning Britain*. The early *TV-am* team of presenters were David Frost, Michael Parkinson, Angela Rippon, Anna Ford, Robert Kee, Esther Rantzen and sports presenter Nick Owen. Anne Diamond joined following a shake up in presenters a few months after the programme was first launched.

The type of television we watched in the evening was changing too. A new style of alternative comedy emerged in the 1980s, showcased in television shows like *The Comic Strip*, *Saturday Live* and *The Young Ones*. There were several new alternative-style comedians including Ben Elton, Jo Brand, Frank Skinner, Alan Davies, Julian Clary and Harry 'Loadsamoney' Enfield. Most of the alternative comedians were about ten years younger than we were and many of us baby boomers just didn't get it. We could appreciate clever satirical comedy but some of us couldn't quite grasp the humour of this new anti-Establishment stuff. Perhaps we were too used to the type of comedy that involved a story and a punchline.

There was a lot of good stuff to watch on television in the 1980s; many excellent writers, producers and directors came to the fore, and there was now little evidence of scenery wobbling about as there had been in the early days of television soap operas. The one exception was of course *Acorn Antiques*, Victoria Wood's wonderful mid-1980s spoof TV soap opera. The choice of television programmes had never been greater; our screens were awash with a multitude of good quality television series and it would be amiss not to highlight some of these wonderful British comedy TV shows, like *'Allo 'Allo!*, *Auf Wiedersehen, Pet*, *Blackadder*, *Bread*, *Hi-de-Hi!*, *Only Fools and Horses* and *Yes, Minister*. We were also spoilt with an abundance of British crime and whodunit TV dramas, like *Bergerac*, *The Bill*, *C.A.T.S. Eyes*, *The Gentle Touch*, *Inspector Morse*, *Juliet Bravo*, *Rumpole of the Bailey* and *Taggart* (with Mark McManus). There were scores of good American police and detective TV series, including *Cagney and Lacey*, *Hill Street Blues*, *L.A. Law*, *Magnum, P.I.*, *Miami Vice* and *Quincy, M.E.*. Other popular British-made TV shows included *Blankety Blank*, *Blind Date*, *Bread*, *Brush Strokes*, *Butterflies*, *Casualty*, *Doctor Who*, *Ever Decreasing Circles*, *A Fine Romance*, *Just Good Friends*, *London's Burning*, *Lovejoy*, *Minder*, *Robin's Nest*, *Shelley*, *Surprise Surprise*, *Tenko*, *To the Manor Born* and *Wogan*, the chat show that was on three nights a week in the late 1980s. Television chat shows were very popular but the choice of guest was sometimes questionable, especially when the guests included glove puppets such as Spit the Dog, Basil Brush and Rod Hull's Emu. The big British-made TV soaps of the day were *Coronation Street*, *Crossroads*, *Eastenders* and *Emmerdale Farm* (as it was called back then). The notable American imports included *Knight Rider*, *The Fall Guy*, *Knots Landing*, *Lou Grant*, *The Cosby Show*, *Moonlighting*, *Mission Impossible*, *Remington Steele*, *Roseanne*, *T. J. Hooker*, *Taxi*, *Fame*, *Hart to Hart*, *Cheers* and of course, the two big ones, *Dallas* and *Dynasty*.

Apart from the 1981 wedding of Charles and Diana, the most-watched television shows of the decade were all episodes from either soaps or situation comedies. The 1986 Christmas episode of *Eastenders* topped the list; the royal wedding was next and then came *Coronation Street*, *Dallas*, *To The Manor Born*, *Bread*, *Neighbours* and *Just Good Friends*. The BBC1 News broadcast from 25 November 1984 managed to sneak in at number nine most watched, and the 1989 Christmas Day episode of *Only Fools and Horses* reached number ten in the ratings. Overall, there were an enormous number of memorable 1980s television shows and it is difficult to choose which ones to mention and which to leave out as any omissions are bound to include someone's favourite. The same goes for films; there was a whole raft of good ones released during the 1980s, far too many to mention individually. Notable British ones include *Chariots of Fire*, *Gandhi*, *Educating Rita*,*Mona Lisa*, *Hope and Glory*, *The Last Emperor*, *My Left Foot*, *Scandal* and *Shirley Valentine*; not to mention the five *James Bond* films that were released in the 1980s. There was an exceptionally large number of big box-office American films of the day and these included *Airplane!*, *The Blues Brothers*, *Fame*, *E.T.*, *Beverly Hills Cop*, *Back to the Future*, *Top Gun*, *Crocodile Dundee*, *Fatal Attraction*, *Batman*, *Ghostbusters*, *Dirty Dancing*, *Die Hard* and of course the *Indiana Jones* films. Whether on television at home or at the cinema, we were certainly not short of good stuff to watch. Unfortunately, we had to wait until the end of the 1990s before we could buy and rent films on DVD.

The popularity of big venue rock and pop concerts of the 1960s and 1970s continued to grow in the 1980s and it was no surprise that Bob Geldof and Midge Ure chose this type of money-making event as the best way to raise money to aid the Ethiopian famine relief. The event they organised was held on 13 July 1985 and it was called Live Aid, which consisted of two huge, dual-venue live concerts. The main concert was held at London's Wembley Stadium and the other was held at the John F. Kennedy Stadium in Philadelphia, USA. These pop/rock concerts were staged as a follow-up to the successful multi-artist charity single that Geldof and Ure had produced for sale over the Christmas period of 1984; a very catchy tune with an extremely moving message, the song was called 'Do They Know It's Christmas?'. On that memorable day in July 1985, Live Aid became a global event with other smaller concerts being held in such places as Australia, Germany, Russia, the Netherlands and Yugoslavia. Prince Charles and Princess Diana officially opened the worldwide charity rock concert from the stage at Wembley Stadium and the BBC television pictures were beamed around the world, to be viewed by 1.5 billion people in 160 countries in the biggest broadcast ever known. The two main concerts at the Wembley and JFK Stadiums featured most of what was considered to be the royalty of pop and rock music, including members of the British baby boomer generation within the line-up of bands, such as The Boomtown Rats, Dire Straits, Queen, Status Quo and Ultravox, and solo artist baby boomers such as David Bowie, Phil Collins, Elton John and Sting. The Who were also there but only the drummer, Kenney Jones, can be classed as a post-war baby boomer; Roger Daltrey and Pete Townsend are too old, having been born during the Second World War, as was Paul McCartney who appeared in the Wembley finale, and Eric Clapton and Mick Jagger who both featured in the JFK concert. It should make all baby boomers feel quite sprightly to be reminded that they are in fact younger than these rock superstars, many of whom were still performing in 2012. Amazingly, Phil Collins managed to perform live in the two main Live Aid concerts on either side of the Atlantic. He did this by boarding a supersonic Concorde flight from the London to New York straight after his performance at Wembley Stadium. Live Aid raised a total of £40 million with half the money spent on food and the other half on long-term development. In those days of high unemployment and job insecurity the spirit of British generosity was clear to see, as whole families queued one after the other to use the house phone (few people had mobiles then) to give their credit card details to volunteers tending special Live Aid donation phone lines at call centres around the country.

But we weren't just watching television every minute of our spare time. In the home, we were busy sanding the varnish from our floors and stripping paint from the woodwork to reveal real pine floorboards, doors and stair rails. We bought loads of solid pine furniture and decorated our rooms with Laura Ashley-style miniature floral-patterned wallpapers and fabrics. We ripped out all of those 1970s coloured bathroom suites and damp bathroom carpets and replaced them with classic white suites and ceramic floor tiles. Those of us lucky enough to have a garage painted over the purple garage doors using more subtle colours. At last, we were bringing style and good taste back into our homes. By the end of the decade our homes had been completely restyled to resemble times gone by but in a very bright and cheery fashion with country cottage kitchens, dado rails and pretty patterned wallpapers. To add to our satisfaction, we were doing it all ourselves. The do-it-yourself (DIY) home improvement craze was now approaching its peak and the companies that had opened high street DIY stores in the early 1970s, many in old cinemas, were now opening huge shed-like DIY superstores in the retail parks, and they usually occupied the largest and most prominent sites available. More and more new-style business and retail parks and shopping malls were being built on out-of-town sites and in inner city disused industrial areas, and DIY stores always featured prominently. There were lots of successful DIY companies around at the time and many became household names. They included B&Q, Do It All, Dodge City, Fads, Focus, Great Mills, Home Charm, Homebase, LCP, Payless, Texas and Wickes. Most of these old names have long since disappeared, having been taken over or shut down over the years, but these were all big retailing names of the 1980s and we spent lots of our money in these stores buying all sorts of DIY products to improve our homes. In some cases it was less of a do-up and more of a botch-up, as many a homebuyer has discovered to their cost since those daft days when thousands of DIY fanatics all across the country could be heard practising their amateur skills late into the night during every weekend and holiday period. They were ever-ready with their electric drill in hand, like a coiled spring waiting to burst into action.

It was during the 1980s that we first began to feel some level of hostility towards our friendly neighbourhood postman. As each year went by we found more and more junk mail littering our doormats, promoting everything from double glazing to foreign holidays, and a lot of it was being delivered by the postman in personally addresses envelopes. It was a fairly new experience for us, something we were not used to, and certainly not on this scale. We regularly got letters telling us that we had won a fortune – we just had to phone a special number to make our claim. Credit card companies bombarded us with part-filled application forms with letters advising us that we had been specially selected to receive one of their credit cards – even gold and platinum cards. We ended up with so many different credit cards that we had to buy special purses and wallets to accommodate them all. Unknown to us, we were becoming targeted consumers. Large companies were gathering information about us and using it to target us for all sorts of consumer products and services. They also began to phone us and use high-pressure sales techniques to sell us their specially priced offers. And guess what? These offers were exclusive for you, and you had to commit to buy them there and then to get the special exclusive prices. These telemarketing companies even sold on our personal information to other marketing companies so that they too could send us mountains of junk mail. We were categorised by these marketing companies and these target categories were given acronym names like Dinky (short for a couple with 'double income no kids yet'). This was certainly the age of consumerism. Each and every one of us was fitted into one category or another and there was a special name to describe every section of society from Tweenies (between 5 and 12 years old) to Empty Nesters (couples whose children have grown up and gone). We weren't very happy with the amount of junk mail and telemarketing phone calls we were getting in the 1980s but we had no idea how bad it was going to get – and we were yet to experience the wonders of the Internet and all the junk mail that would create. In the early 1980s, we in Britain had seen the arrival of the first home computers with such makes as Apple, Apricot, Amstrad, Commodore, IBM and Sinclair, who made the ZX Spectrum, Britain's best-selling computer, but we would have to wait until the 1990s to experience the Internet and email messaging.

The 1980s was the decade in which we saw the birth of young upwardly mobile professionals, or yuppies as they were more commonly known. These were high-earning young professionals who were totally absorbed in their own world of opulent living and completely out of touch with ordinary life. City traders working on the financial markets in London's financial Square Mile were earning huge salaries and bonuses and they characterised the British yuppie image to the extreme. They were mostly under 30 with fully loaded gold and platinum credit cards that were burning holes in their pockets. They developed a reputation for being shameless in their unbounded spending on lavish champagne lunches costing hundreds of pounds a time, and for leaving tips that were large enough to feed an average family for a week. They bought all of the expensive trappings that you associate with ostentatious rich people (or flash gits, as many less-privileged mortals were inclined to call them). They spent money like there was no tomorrow. Top of the range Porsches and gold Rolex watches seemed to be among the essential parts of their kit. They took to wearing wide-striped braces in a style that was perfectly portrayed by Gordon Gekko's character in the 1987 film, *Wall Street*. They used the 'work hard and play hard' ethic to explain their brash overspending, but the whole culture was generally viewed as being an unbridled feast of self-indulgence. Many young people were attracted to the yuppie image and the desire for such a lifestyle became contagious. Soon other young professionals were imitating the city high flyers, albeit to a lesser extent. Business executives throughout the land bought leather-bound Filofax personal organiser wallets, the must-have yuppie accessory before the days of electronic organisers. They stuffed their Filofax wallets with as many loose-leaf pages as they could possibly fit in; the bulgier the Filofax the more important they looked. As with any fashion trend, there were a lot of wannabes: less-wealthy young people who couldn't afford to keep pace with the true yuppies but still wanted to be seen as part of the yuppie set. Many were willing to get themselves into debt just so they could hang around expensive wine bars and at least look the part. Fortunately, by then most of us baby boomers were a little too old to be cast as stereotypical, young, upwardly mobile professionals, and so perhaps we can rest easy in the knowledge that we played no part in the culture of extreme greed and self-indulgence that was linked to the yuppie lifestyle of the 1980s. Well, at least some of us can.

The worldwide stock market crash of 1987 instantly restrained the extravagant spending habits of the city whiz kid yuppies. The wine bars, restaurants and clubs that the high-spending yuppies had previously heaped money upon soon came creeping back to ordinary Joe Public to fill their tills. Venues that had previously been standoffish to all but the big spenders suddenly threw their doors open to welcome all-comers in the face of fierce competition to fill empty tables and floor space.

As was the case in previous decades, the 1980s is remembered for having some very distinctive styles of dress.

The passage of time does tend to play tricks with our minds and, as such, we have a tendency to arrogantly mock bygone clothing fashions. We cringe at the thought that we could ever have worn such things, and the 1980s do not escape ridicule from today's critics. Whatever you might think of the fashion trends, the 1980s must surely go down in the annals of history as having been a much more tasteful and stylish period than the early to mid-1970s. The large shoulder pads, tight jeans and leg warmers of the 1980s really weren't that bad. Okay, so the mullet hair cut did reach the peak of its popularity in the 1980s and there was an early trend for men to perm their hair to look as if they had a poodle sat on their head. Oh, and yes in the late 1980s some men did take to wearing short ponytails for a while. Even back then, most of us thought that these were all awful hairstyles and the majority of us were sensible enough to trim our 1970s locks into much smarter hairstyles, and generally smarten ourselves up. Power dressing was the slogan of the day. The elegant Armani suits and high-collared lace blouses of the 1980s must make up for all of the chavvy shell suits, ripped sweatshirts, rah-rah skirts and Lycra leggings that we saw parading through our shopping centres at the weekends. There were a lot of classic styles around but we tend to overlook these and concentrate on the fashion faux pas. Many of us wore expensive and well-tailored clothes but we sometimes wore them in a strange way; like the designer jackets worn with sleeves hitched up to the elbows and a casual t-shirt underneath, in the style of the 1980s *Miami Vice* TV series. Brand names became status symbols and designer labels began to appear on everything we bought from sportswear to luggage. We willingly paid ten-times the price of a cotton t-shirt to get one that was printed with a designer name or logo emblazoned across the front. Gone were the days when companies had to pay to have their logos displayed on the high street. We consumers were now paying them for the privilege of flaunting their brands everywhere we went. It became fashionable to wear wax cotton jackets in town, especially Barbour jackets, and when it was wet a matching pair of green Hunter wellington boots. They gave the impression that you were up from the country for the day. This was also the decade in which the term Sloane Ranger first came into use to describe the wealthy, young, upper-class set that lived in the Chelsea area of London and were regularly seen shopping in and around Sloane Square. The Sloane Ranger tag was mostly applied to the women of the Chelsea set who invariably had cut-glass English accents and family estates in the country; a prime example was Diana, Princess of Wales, or Lady Diana Spencer as she was before her marriage to Charles, Prince of Wales. There was even an official Sloane Ranger Handbook and a Sloane Ranger Diary, both published by the magazine *Harpers & Queen*. Meanwhile, there was an unusual change going on in everyday footwear. While we baby boomers continued to wear our highly polished leather shoes, all around us the younger generation were binning the tradition and formality of leather shoes in favour of new-style designer trainers from the likes of Nike and Reebok. To the young, these designer trainers were now acceptable for everyday use, to be worn with anything and on any occasion. Some children were now growing up having never worn anything else on their feet but sports trainers. It was difficult for us, the plimsoll generation of the 1950s, to adjust to such a radical change in everyday footwear. How could anyone wear casual trainers with a suit or a dress and expect to be taken seriously? We baby boomers would never do that, would we? Surely, we could never become that tacky.

Having joined one of the thousands of newly opened gyms in the 1970s and taken up jogging as well, we were certainly buying gym shoes in greater numbers than ever before. Our interest in keep fit was proving to be more than just a short-lived fad. Women were especially keen to trim and tone their figures, which for those of our generation were not quite as young and trim as they used to be. Spurred on by 1980s dance-themed films like *Fame*, *Staying Alive*, and *Flashdance*, armies of women of all ages were donning headbands, leotards and leg warmers and joining aerobic classes at dance studios and church halls throughout the land. Home fitness videos topped their Christmas wish lists, especially the Jane Fonda workout videos and the *Physical* video by Olivia Newton John. We may have taken up jogging in the 1970s in an attempt to get fit, but this was now serious stuff – we were even signing up to run marathons (the London Marathon and the Great North Run half marathon were first staged in 1981).

It was as well that we were toning our bodies and increasing oxygen to our brains because we would need all of the energy and brain power we could muster to keep us going as we left the 1980s behind us and moved on into the 1990s, with the bleak prospects of further falls in house prices and increasing numbers of repossessions, high interest rates and rising inflation. The decade ended on a high note with news from Germany that East Germany's communist rulers had given permission for the gates of the Berlin Wall to be opened. On 9 November 1989, for the first time since 1961, the 28 mile wall was officially breached and hundreds of East Berliners surged through the openings while large numbers of jubilant West Berliners climbed to the top of the wall and began breaking up sections of it.

1990s

Pass the Reading Glasses

Whene we closed the door on the 1980s we ushered out much of what remained of the good old-fashioned Britishness that symbolised our traditional way of life. In the past, evolution of gadgets had been a gradual process but towards the end of the 1980s new technology was really starting to speed things up. Once underway, the impetus could only get faster as technology continued to develop more and more new and better gadgets to improve ways of doing everything, whether in the workplace or at home. From communications to cooking, technology was fundamentally changing our traditional way of life as increasing numbers of people of every age group made use of each and every new gadget as soon as it became available. During the 1990s everything was changing and developing at breathtaking speed. It may have been an involuntary act but by buying into the technological age we were altering our whole way of life, and in a very short space of time. As we look back, we probably remember the 1980s as being the last decade that was not totally dominated by electronic gadgetry in one form or another. From mass ownership of mobile phones to nationwide CCTV surveillance cameras in our streets, shops, workplaces and buildings, the rapid advancements in technology during the 1990s was exciting and most of us were unable to resist the temptation of joining this new high-tech society, thus drawing us ever closer towards a twenty-first-century lifestyle and taking us further and further away from the world of pen and paper in which we grew up.

The first major world event we remember from the decade was Nelson Mandela's release from a South African prison on 11 February 1990 after serving twenty-seven years of a life sentence. The event is high on our list of memories from the early 1990s because it dominated all forms of media coverage and his release was broadcast live on television all over the world. In Britain there were also some vitally important things happening that were changing the structure of our nation. Our minds are easily transported back to the early days of the 1990s if we are reminded of when, in May 1990, the then minister of agriculture, John Gummer, invited newspaper and television camera crews to photograph him trying to feed a beef burger to his 4-year-old daughter in an attempt to reassure the public that British beef was safe for humans to eat, despite concerns about mad cow disease (BSE) in cattle.

His daughter refused to eat any of the burger and he was left to sample it for himself. However, the biggest news story that year was the resignation of Margaret Thatcher as prime minister and leader of the Conservative Party in November 1990. She decided to go after she only narrowly won a leadership contest against Michael Heseltine. This made her realise that she no longer had the overwhelming support of her MPs and so she stood down. Margaret Thatcher had been the leader of the Conservative Party for fifteen years and prime minister for eleven; this made her the longest-serving British prime minister of the twentieth century. Following Thatcher's resignation, the then chancellor of the exchequer, John Major, was elected leader of the Conservative Party and he became prime minister.

The Queen celebrated her Ruby Jubilee on 6 February 1992, but aside from that the early 1990s were a difficult and painful time for her and the royal family was never far away from controversy. The failing marriages of three of the Queen's children – Prince Charles, Prince Andrew and Princess Anne – and the shame of seeing tabloid, front-page scandal pictures of her daughter-in-law, the Duchess of York (Sarah Ferguson), were all a great disappointment to the Queen, but there was even more distress to come. In November 1992, Windsor Castle was badly damaged by a fire that caused more than £50 million worth of damage. At the same time, it was announced that the Queen was to start paying tax the following year. She described 1992 as being *Annus Horribilis* (a Latin phrase for 'horrible year'). In 1994, the Duchess of Kent became the first member of the royal family for more than 300 years to convert to Catholicism. In May 1996, the Duke and Duchess of York divorced, and in August that year, after four years of separation, Prince Charles and Princess Diana divorced. It was certainly a difficult period for the royal family and the biggest upset was yet to come. Just one year after the divorce, on 31 August 1997, much of the world went into mourning when news reached us that Princess Diana had been killed in a car crash in Paris. This was the biggest and most shocking news event of the decade, an occasion that will be forever fixed in the minds of everyone who was around at the time. She was greatly admired and loved by people from all over the world.

In 1994, for the first time in history, Britain had a direct link to France via a tunnel beneath the English Channel: the Eurotunnel. In 1998, we saw a devolved government established in Scotland, an assembly in Wales, and a legislature in Northern Ireland; this was effectively a breakdown of powers and decision making that was previously controlled from London by the Parliament of the United Kingdom of Great Britain and Northern Ireland. This was the first tangible evidence of a divide in our nation and it prepared the ground for the possible future breaking up of the four countries of the United Kingdom. In particular, there were pressure groups in Scotland and Wales in favour of seeking greater autonomy or even independence from the rest of the UK. The situation in Northern Ireland was somewhat different with the main argument being whether Northern Ireland should become part of a united Ireland or remain in the United Kingdom. Following agreements made during the 1990s Northern Ireland peace process, any change in Northern Ireland's sovereignty would only be allowed to happen with the agreement of a majority of voters in both Northern Ireland and the Republic of Ireland. Meanwhile, the 50-million population of England who accounted for the majority of the UK's population watched on quietly from the side lines as nationalist battles went on all around. The reallocation of responsibilities and management of different budgets brought many issues into question, not least the possibility of a break-up of the National Health Service and an end to fair and equal national policies on our healthcare. In 1999, the peace deal for Northern Ireland, known as The Good Friday Agreement, came into force and the new Euro currency was launched in participating European countries, but not in Britain because we chose to keep the pound sterling as our main currency.

It was increasingly apparent that little mainland Britain was becoming somewhat overcrowded and the growing population was putting a great strain on all of our social welfare and utility services, especially housing, schools and the National Health Service. It was also very noticeable that our country was becoming more cosmopolitan with an even greater ethnic mix of people using a multitude of different languages. Figures from the Office of National Statistics show that in the early 1990s there was little difference between the number of people entering the UK and those leaving, but immigration began to increase significantly in 1994 and the trend continued throughout the remainder of the 1990s with immigrant numbers exceeding emigrants by about 25%. During the decade, the total UK population rose by 1.3 million to a figure of just under 59 million by the end of 1999. It did seem like our country was becoming overpopulated and there was an increasing number of people needing social welfare.

The nation's addiction to watching television was getting worse. We were growing increasing fond of trivia programmes, especially soap operas, fly-on-the-wall documentaries and TV reality shows featuring ordinary people. A large section of viewers were finding it difficult to separate fact from fiction when watching these shows. In fact, many *Eastenders* fans from outside of the London area believed that real East-enders actually behaved as they were portrayed each evening on the fictional TV show. As if any group of neighbours could spend their whole lives bickering and shouting at one another, let alone people from the East End area of London who have a long-standing reputation for their warm and friendly nature.

The Spice Girls pop group were at the height of their popularity in the mid- to late 1990s. 'Girl power' and 'celebrity' were the buzzwords. Children and teenagers no longer dreamed of becoming nurses and train drivers as we baby boomers did when we were young. All of a sudden, everyone wanted to be on television so they could be a celebrity. Having no talent whatsoever was no longer an obstacle to stardom. Some wanted to be singers and actors but many just craved the limelight that came with being a celebrity. It seemed that you could now be famous for just having been on television. Many kids thought that 'celebrity' was a job title in itself. Appearing in a reality television show qualified you as a television personality and a Z-list celebrity. You would even be asked to make personal appearances, to open shops and switch on the Christmas lights in your local town centre. We were entering a new dream world where naïve youngsters were being misled into believing that it was possible for everyone to make a living in the world of pop music and television, and celebrity status was within everyone's grasp. What a great world that would be, if we were all able to turn a hobby into a job, but how would the world survive? Who would keep the wheels turning? The attraction of reality television shows and the adoration of anyone who even hinted celebrity status was growing and we would see it escalate a few years down the line with the arrival of TV talent contest shows such as *Pop Idol*, *Fame Academy*, and *X Factor*, as well as the infamous *Big Brother* reality game show television series.

Whatever our own personal choice of television viewing might have been, by the early 1990s those of us who could afford the high monthly fees were watching the new multi-channel Sky Television. Unfortunately, we had to wait until the 1998 for the all-digital service to start, and of course we had to pay more for the receiver and for the extra channels that came with it, but Sky Television came into our living rooms promising us a choice of hundreds of television channels of quality digital viewing. However, we soon discovered there were only about ten channels worth watching and those included the mainstream BBC and ITV channels that were still available to watch free of charge using the old terrestrial analogue aerial. We also had to pay extra one-off fees on top of the huge monthly subscription charges if we wanted to watch recently released movies, some football matches and special sporting events like the big boxing contests. From March 1997, we had another national terrestrial analogue free-to-view channel to watch following the launch of Channel 5. This was the first new TV channel in the UK since the launch of Channel 4 in November 1982. We now had five free-to-view national terrestrial analogue networks and there were to be no more because all future new channels would be digital.

The top five most-watched, individual television shows of the 1990s (excluding sports, special events and news programmes) were *Only Fools and Horses* ('Time on Our Hands', 1996 Christmas episode with 24.35 million viewers), *Eastenders* (2 January 1992, with 24.3 million viewers including repeat showing), *Panorama*, interview of Princess Diana by Martin Bashir on 20 November 1995 following her separation from Prince Charles (22.78 million viewers), *Coronation Street* (episode screened on 8 January 1992 with 21.60 million viewers), and the *Neighbours* episode shown on 26 February 1990, which attracted 21.16 million viewers including repeat. These were all BBC programmes apart from *Coronation Street*, which was on the ITV (Granada) network. The Christmas 1996 episode of *Only Fools and Horses*, in which Del Boy and Rodney Trotter finally become millionaires is, as at 2010, the most watched non-documentary or event programme of all time in the UK. Topping the list of most-watched special events was of course the funeral of Diana, Princess of Wales, which had

32.10 million viewers (BBC/ITV) on 6 September 1997. The second most-watched special event of the 1990s was the World Cup 1998 football match when England played Argentina on 30 June 1998. The then 18-year-old Michael Owen scored a stunning goal and David Beckham was sent off for kicking Diego Simeone; 23.78 million British television viewers (ITV) saw England lose 4-3 on penalties after drawing the match 2–2.

Other popular television shows of the 1990s included *Alright on the Night*, *Auntie's Bloomers*, *Birds of a Feather*, *Inspector Morse* and *London's Burning*. A great many new television programmes also arrived during the decade. These included an abundance of comedy series, such as *2point4 Children* (1991), *Dinnerladies* (1998), *Men Behaving Badly* (1992), *Have I Got News For You?* (1990), *One Foot in the Grave* (1990), *The Royle Family* (1998) and *The Vicar of Dibley* (1994). There was the gentle humour of programmes like *As Time Goes By* (1992), *Ballykissangel* (1996), *Darling Buds of May* (1991) and *Goodnight Sweetheart* (1993), and lots of drama mysteries and police series such as *A Touch of Frost* (1992), *Dalziel and Pascoe* (1996), *Hamish Macbeth* (1995), *Heartbeat* (1992), *Jonathan Creek* (1997), *Kavanagh QC* (1995), *Midsomer Murders* (1997), *Prime Suspect* (1991) and *Wycliffe* (1993). There were also gentle dramas like *The House of Eliott* (1991) and *Where The Heart Is* (1997), and lots of light entertainment shows such as *Barrymore* (1991), *Noel's House Party* (1991) and *You've Been Framed* (1990). There was a plentiful assortment of DIY and gardening programmes in the vein of *DIY SOS* (1999), *Changing Rooms* (1996) and *Ground Force* (1997), and it was also the decade in which we were first introduced to the hugely popular television quiz show *Who Wants to be a Millionaire?* (1998), the competitive sports-like game show *Gladiators* (1992) and the children's favourite of that era, *Teletubbies* (1997).

Elsewhere in the home, instead of using our conventional ovens we were saving time by cooking more microwaveable meals, and the time we saved we put into doing trendy DIY projects like garden decking, which was a real craze in the late 1990s and into the 2000s. An increasing number of us were now also computer literate, investing in personal computers to use at home, and by the late 1990s we were connecting to the Internet and communicating with friends and family all over the world by email messaging. By that time, most of us also had a mobile phone and these were getting smaller and smaller with more and more functions, and the good news was that they were also getting more affordable.

By the late 1990s, we were selling our collections of VHS films at car boot sales and buying remastered versions in the new DVD format – yet another new machine to buy! Video games and home video game consoles were becoming hugely popular with children and adults alike, and these very expensive video game consoles were at the top of the must-have list of Christmas presents, at least for anyone under the age of about 35. These were all a bit too hi-tech for the rest of us but many did at least have a go on one of what the techies called the fifth-generation consoles, these being the likes of the Sega Saturn, Sony's PlayStation and the Nintendo 64. We had to wait another couple of years for the Xbox to go on sale – as if we cared!

By now, most of us baby boomers had long since given up listening to what we now regarded as 'noise' on BBC Radio 1 and we had switched our allegiance to easier-on-the-ear stations like Radio 2 or Radio 3. Some of us preferred to alternate between a number of news and current affairs radio stations, such as BBC Radio 4 and Radio 5 Live, or perhaps one or two of the independent broadcasters like the national Talk Radio (now Talk Sport) or a local radio station like London's LBC Radio. Whatever our choice of listening, even if by then we had lost all interest in pop music, we couldn't help but notice the word Britpop being bandied around by the media. This was a tag given to some of the British guitar bands of the 1990s, including Blur, Oasis, Pulp, Radiohead, Suede, Supergrass and The Verve. Even the most out of touch and closeted among us will at least have heard these names and know that they were among the leading pop music-makers of the 1990s. Some of us even liked the stuff they produced. The main point being that, as ever, British pop music was alive and well in the 1990s and there were an abundance of British music makers flying the flag all around the world, especially in America; these included people like Elton John, George Michael, Phil Collins and Sting. Oh, and remember BRIT Awards winner 1991/92 – Lisa Stansfield?

The scene on our high streets had been slowly changing since the 1960s. By the beginning of the 1990s the traditional high street was becoming unrecognisable. The huge edge-of-town supermarkets were increasing in numbers, as were the out-of-town retail parks that boasted all the big-name department stores and retail chains. These enormous shed-like stores were enticing more and more customers away from the high street with promises of vast choices of merchandise, competitively priced products and free and easy parking, often promoted through television and newspaper advertising campaigns. New supermarket names were opening large numbers of stores across the country. In 1990, the German-owned Aldi discount supermarket chain opened its first British superstore in Birmingham (as of 2012 they have 421 stores in the UK); that same year, the British variety store Poundland opened its first store in Burton-upon-Trent, selling everything at £1 per item (as of 2009 they have 250 stores in the UK); also in 1990, the Swedish discount food supermarket chain Netto opened their first British store in Leeds (147 UK stores by 2010 when ASDA took over Netto UK and rebranded the stores). In 1991, we saw the first British retail computer superstore, PC World, open in Croydon, Surrey (they had 206 UK stores by 2006). Some long-established high street names were also disappearing during the 1990s. These included Rumbelows, the electrical goods retailer, whose name vanished in 1995 when owners, Thorn EMI, shut the remaining 285 Rumbelows stores. The Midland Bank name also ceased to exist after 163 years on the high street when in 1999 the bank adopted the name of its owner, HSBC.

Encouraged by offers from large national retailers to pay for new access roads, local councils cheerfully approved and even encouraged the building of new superstores in their local areas. They even put up signs directing motorists to the new superstores and away from the small high-street shops. At the same time as they were steering customers away from the high street and into the free car parks of the edge-of-town supermarkets, the local councils were busy painting more and more yellow lines on our roads and erecting increasing amounts of road signage. In 1992, the first fixed-site speed cameras were installed. There was no evidence that they reduced road traffic accidents but the fines they generated provided yet another source of revenue; very soon they were everywhere. By now, all government and police departments had come to regard the motorists as easy-target cash cows and this type of action was seen as a very certain, long-term way of generating a steady, dependable flow of cash. New red routes and bus lanes were being created, primarily in and around the London area, and traffic wardens were being given targets to issue certain numbers of tickets each day to help swell the coffers with as many fines as possible. Traffic wardens found they needed to adopt devious methods to achieve their high targets, like hiding in shop doorways to catch any unsuspecting motorist who might leave a car outside a shop for a minute. They would even stand next to parking meters waiting for the allotted times to run out so that they could immediately issue tickets before the owners could get back to their cars. Motorists were being terrorised by increasing numbers of brutish enforcers who were engaged by the local councils to clamp or tow away unauthorised or illegally parked vehicles, even those that were only breaching minor parking regulations. These clamping firms would then menacingly extract huge sums of cash, described as fees, from the vehicle owner before they would undertake to remove a wheel clamp or release an offending vehicle from their council-approved vehicle pound. It was a sort of legalised extortion, all done in the cause of keeping obstructing vehicles off the streets to keep traffic flowing. The fact that drivers were unable to drive away an obstructing vehicle until the fine was paid and the wheel clamp removed didn't seem to matter to the congestion-conscious officials, even though the process was not a quick one and sometimes not dealt with the same day. These observations were not deemed to be important, just as long as the money kept rolling in. There was even talk of introducing a new tax on vehicles entering and driving around city centres, but of course if that happened it would only be done for the purpose of reducing congestion and pollution, not to raise revenue – No! That would just be a fortunate by-product of any such scheme.

Meanwhile, back in the high streets, no mercy was being shown towards the ever-reducing number of small traditional retailers that were trying to survive in the dying town centres all over the country. The exorbitant business rates and waste disposal charges continued to rise each year. Every month, thousands of small retail shops were giving up and closing their doors for the last time. Many of these were long-established family businesses that had been part of a town's lifeblood for generations, and they were being forced out of business because of modern retailing with superstores and shopping malls stocking everything under one roof. The downfall of the high street was not the fault of online shopping; competition from that facility was yet to come. Indeed, online shopping would add to the problems of retailing in years to come but shopping over the Internet didn't start in the UK until the mid-1990s and even then it was very limited. It didn't really get going here until the late 1990s when the likes of Amazon began to make it easy and secure for us to do credit card transactions online. In the meantime, it was the diversification and growth of the large retailing groups that was sucking the life out of the high street as we once knew it. The final straw for high street trading came when Sunday trading was legalised in England and Wales in 1994. Many of the large superstore retailers in England and Wales had been opening illegally on Sundays, off and on, since the mid-1980s because the fines were much lower than their Sunday profits, but now it was legal and they could go all out to make Sunday the second most popular shopping day of the week after Saturday. Scotland was unaffected by the change because they never had any general legislation regarding Sunday trading. Many of our large centres began to resemble war zones with row upon row of boarded-up shops only broken by the occasional bank, building society, betting shop, take-away food shop and a growing number of charity shops. The number of real retailers that were actually selling goods was becoming too few to attract enough shoppers to keep the traditional high street alive. We certainly bought into the comfort and convenience of shopping malls and superstores and there was no stopping the trend, but at the same time we needed to find a new use for our once-busy high streets and market squares to stop them turning into ghost towns and becoming no-go areas for all but the new-style of hooded youths (hoodies) and other sinister layabouts. Their menacing presence only added to the run-down appearance of these places and made us feel unsafe to go there anymore. Sadly, nobody was paying any attention to the problem and so our once-cherished town centres continued to deteriorate with each passing year.

The breakdown in law and order on the streets of Britain, particularly with rebellious young people and problem families causing trouble and destroying property, led to the introduction of Anti-Social Behaviour Orders (ASBOs) in 1998. They were effectively an official slap on the wrist for persistent offenders but they became a must-have badge of honour for the people they were supposed to bring to heel. Controlling the activities of criminals was to get even more difficult in years to come, after the Human Rights Act received Royal Assent in 1998 (came into force in 2000), when every criminal and preacher of hatred would be able to use the act to seek protection from the law for one fanciful reason or another.

We had grown accustomed to accelerating house prices in the 1980s and seen big rises in property values. Many homeowners believed this was an on-going trend and that their money was safely invested in their property, which was proving to be a fantastic investment. On the strength of this, many had funded their spending by borrowing money against the value of their homes. Some took advantage of the situation, selling their homes for profit and taking out larger mortgages to buy more expensive properties before the prices of those properties increased beyond their reach. However, towards the end of the 1980s it all started to go wrong; mortgage interest rates had risen from 9% in 1988 to an exorbitant 14%, and they stayed at that level until late 1992. Just to rub salt in the festering wound, house prices were now falling at an alarming rate. In the space of just a few months, average house prices had fallen by 5% to £59,587 (March 1990). Thereafter, they continued to fall steadily month by month and they did not begin to recover until the mid-1990s, by which time they had reached a low of £50,930 at 1995 prices. In a little under six years the average price of a house in the UK fell by £11,852 at 1995 values and during that period many house owners found themselves in negative equity, having bought their property when prices were much higher.

Along with every other unfortunate homeowner in the UK, we baby boomers were not only suffering the headache of living in negative equity properties that were still falling in value, but we also had to find increasing amounts of money each month to pay the sky-high mortgage interest rates. The overall level of consumer debt was rising but our wage packets were only so big and many homeowners found they could not afford the mortgage repayments; many of those who could were often living off the back of credit cards. This, together with the 1989–90 sharp rises in inflation, led to a dramatic rise in mortgage arrears, which resulted in a big increase in property repossessions in the early 1990s. Some homeowners who could no longer afford to meet their monthly mortgage payments and were also unable to realise the loan amount through the sale of their property were actually going into their building society lender branches and handing over their house keys to the counter staff. Homeowners in expensive areas of the country such as London and the South East found they were laden with huge mortgage debts on properties that were worth tens (and in some cases hundreds) of thousands of pounds less than they paid for them. Ordinary working-class families were suffering the burden of having significant negative equity in their family homes. It was not uncommon for such families to have a £120,000 mortgage on a house that was worth less than £100,000. In spring 1990, the country was in recession and inflation had reached 9.4%, the highest level for eight years. Everyone was feeling the pinch and some a great deal more than others. A lot of families became homeless and turned to local authorities and charities to provide them with temporary accommodation. Those were desperate times for anyone trying to pay off any kind of debt in the days of exceptionally high interest rates. Although the government did encourage the moneylenders to be sympathetic to loan defaulters during those difficult times, sympathy was not a typical banker's trait and the bailiffs were never short of work. People living in rented accommodation did not avoid the pain either; they too suffered the effects of the increasing costs of living. Many had been left saddled with debts they incurred when unemployment was at its peak in the mid-1980s. Although unemployment levels had been falling during the previous three years, the numbers were now rising again, and they were rising rapidly. By December 1991, unemployment was above 2.5 million for the first time since early 1988. Evictions due to mortgage and rent arrears were on the increase as we moved through the 1990s, and there was more bad news to come; in his 1993 budget, Chancellor Norman Lamont announced plans to introduce a Value Added Tax (VAT) on domestic electric and gas bills at a rate of 8% for 1994 and 17.5% for 1995 and thereafter. Fortunately, by spring 1993 the country was coming out the three-year recession and inflation was back under control, down to a twenty-nine-year low of 1.3% and then floating between 1.5% and 3% for the rest of the 1990s. As for property prices, they continued to fall until 1995 when the market began to settle, and from 1996 house prices were once more on the rise and we started to experience steady growth again. Nevertheless, the damage had been done, and many families had been badly stung by their experiences in house buying.

The 1990s was the decade in which we became much more aware of the term 'political correctness' (PC), an expression that had been used in its modern form since the 1970s but only among a select few political activists. The term was often used in sarcasm to describe people or organisations that might say or do something just to appear to be doing the right and acceptable thing, even if what they said didn't really represent their true views. Someone who said something just to appease the sensibilities of others might be accused of trying to be 'politically correct'. Conversely, feminists used the term in the 1970s and 1980s when dealing with topics like male chauvinism and sexism. The phrase entered everyday language in the mid-1980s when a number of wacky headline-grabbing stories emerged, many of which were fabricated. It was in 1986 that one of the first of these made up PC stories hit the headlines. A newspaper article claimed that an independent parent-run nursery school in Hackney in London had tried to change the words of the nursery rhyme 'Baa Baa Black Sheep' to 'Baa Baa White Sheep' because the original wording was racist. In the end they were said to have banned the nursery rhyme altogether. The story was later discredited and found to be untrue. It was accepted that although someone at the nursery had suggested the original wording might be considered racist, there was never a ban. However, the story was given credence to run because the then leader of the Hackney Council issued a statement supporting the actions of the nursery school in banning the offending rhyme. The story became national news because what was regarded as a 'loony Left-wing' council had impetuously jumped on the bandwagon and given the story unwarranted credibility. The political correctness epidemic had begun and the term was increasingly used during the late 1980s, gaining momentum in the 1990s. The political correctness doctrine was mainly linked to 'loony Left-wing' councils and other self-appointed airy-fairy, libertarian, political groups, who thought they were superior beings whose duty it was to impose their beliefs on the rest of society and be our hand-wringing moral guardians. Many regarded them as a bunch of yoghurt-knitting do-gooders who, among other things, through their campaigning managed to get the rights of criminals placed above those of their victims. One example of perceived politically correct action being taken against popular opinion was when the Labour-controlled Birmingham City Council renamed Christmas 1998 festivities as 'Winterval'. Although originally intended as a marketing strategy of inclusion, the media inevitably saw it differently. Since the 1990s, the word Christmas has been widely erased from use at Christmastime by many of our local councils in the name of political correctness, and it has been replaced by words and phrases such as wintertime, winter or festival lights and the festive period. We have witnessed an increasing trend for local councils to change traditional Christmas street decorations to new-style displays that symbolise wintertime rather than Christmastime, with lights in the shape of snowflakes and such like. Other examples of how political correctness has gone mad over the years include the jobcentre in Thetford, Norfolk that refused to accept a job advert for a 'reliable and hardworking' applicant because it could be seen as offensive to unreliable and lazy people. There was also the case of Flintshire County Council renaming the classic English pudding, known by all as spotted dick, to 'Spotted Richard' to avoid causing offence. In their wisdom, the BBC did away with comic cartoon rogue Dennis the Menace's bombs, catapult, pea shooter and water pistol as part of a politically correct makeover of Dennis prior to commissioning a new television series.

In the name of equality, the PC brigade set out to make everything gender neutral: a manhole became a maintenance hole; man-made became synthetic; hospital ward sisters became ward managers and a dustman became a waste disposal operative. There were countless numbers of PC name changes; dustman, fireman, fisherman, milkman, policeman, postman, headmaster and headmistress, they were all given new, non-gender-specific titles. Anything that could be construed as being racist was removed; a blackboard became a chalkboard and black coffee was re-described as coffee without milk. While we baby boomers were finding the tidal wave of change hard to contend with, young children were growing up within an already established politically correct system and they were accepting these things as normal, just as they were accepting sport in schools without the competitive element of winners and losers as being normal, and not being allowed to play conkers in case they hurt themselves was also normal for them. We were protecting our children to the nth degree; for example, in nursery schools, 'hide and seek' was renamed 'find who's lost'. We were even beginning to treat children like adults, describing them as young people rather than kids or children. For as many stories of 'political correctness gone mad' that are just urban myths, there are as many again that are factual.

John Major's Conservative government didn't do enough to quell all of the madcap political correctness, and Tony Blair's Labour government of the late 1990s was thought to have added to the problem by excessively kowtowing to minority sensitivities. They seemed to be conforming to politically correct views and even encouraging some of the daft ideas associated with the practice of political correctness. We became too precious, obsessed with using the right words, not to upset anyone, at whatever cost. We were losing the right to speak our minds; political correctness was eroding the freedom of speech that our country had always boasted of, something we baby boomers had grown up with and were used to exercising to its fullest extent. We were expected to change the way we expressed our thoughts and to stop using many of the words and phrases we had used in everyday speech all of our lives. Political correctness seemed to provide a licence for someone to be labelled extreme or prejudice if they said or did something that someone somewhere might consider to be 'politically incorrect'.

Political correctness went hand in glove with the exaggerated use of health and safety rules. Their combined forces seemed intent on interfering with and spoiling our usual way of life. Bureaucrats were becoming obsessed with health and safety regulations, at home and in schools, out on the streets and at work. Especially at work, where it seemed at times that government officials were actually trying to stop businesses from functioning altogether because of the over-the-top way they administered their duties and applied the rules to every area of people's wellbeing. In the 1990s, the whole thing was becoming ridiculous; everything was being made into a health and safety issue. People were frightened to move in case they contravened health and safety regulations. Businesses were being forced to spend vast sums of money to facilitate health and safety requirements in every aspect of the workplace, including buildings, equipment, clothing, record keeping and working practices. Unreasonable health and safety rules were costing jobs. Anything that could possibly cause someone harm was treated as a health and safety issue, even if it wasn't officially the case. Schools were banning long-established playground games for fear that a child might get hurt. The game of British Bulldog was widely banned, as was the playing of conkers without protective masks and gloves. Children were no longer allowed to get hurt. They were increasingly being mollycoddled, growing up without any of the usual cuts and grazes and black eyes that have always been associated with one's childhood. Health and safety was definitely a prime example of bureaucracy gone mad: a sort of job-creation scheme for bureaucrats, which was designed to drive us all crazy and stop us from functioning. This was a typical example of what was coming to be known as the 'nanny state' of Britain. The sad thing is that it was never reigned in and by the end of the 1990s, it was looking unstoppable.

Throughout the 1990s, the streets of Britain were plagued with unrest and disorder. We started the decade with the worrying problem of NHS ambulance crews taking industrial action over pay and conditions at a time when the threat of IRA terrorist attacks hung over our daily lives. The industrial action began back in September 1989 and went on for six long months until a pay agreement was finally reached and the ambulance crews returned to normal working hours in March 1990. In that same year, retail shops around the country were reporting that sales were at their lowest level since 1980 and the CBI confirmed that Britain was once more in recession.

Unemployment was rising sharply and a demonstrable mood of unrest was again evident. The now-familiar sight of disorder and rioting returned to our streets in the early 1990s, especially in London with the famous Poll Tax riots, which only ended when the new prime minister, John Major, announced in April 1991 that the much-hated Community Charge (Poll Tax) was to be abolished and replaced with a new Council Tax in 1993.

There were a large number of terrorist atrocities during the 1990s; various individual fanatics and organisations carried out dozens of terrorist bombings in mainland Britain and in Northern Ireland, killing scores of innocent people and injuring hundreds more.

Ignoring problems with the housing market, inflation and high interest rates of the early-1990s, the average standard of living in Britain during the 1990s was quite high and it was light years away from the lifestyle we experienced back in the post-war austere Britain of the 1940s and 1950s. We now enjoyed possessions and a way of life that was beyond anything imaginable to us forty years earlier. Things that we now took for granted were in fact luxuries but we no longer regarded them as such. The passage of time had turned televisions, telephones, stereos, fridges and domestic freezers into essential household items that we now thought we could not live without. Certainly, the younger generations could not imagine what it was like to live without these items. Each year the choice of luxury goods got bigger and there was now a huge variety of lifestyle-enhancing products and services available to us. We were bombarded with adverts and promotional literature every minute of our waking days. From adverts on hoardings to junk mail, television campaigns to nuisance phone calls; it seemed as though every company in the world was canvassing our business and teasing the money from our pockets.

Having no money was a minor hurdle to overcome because the banks, credit card companies and other moneylenders were falling over themselves to lend us as much as we wanted. If your credit card was already spent up to its limit you could just get another one, or two, or three. In fact, consumerism and money lending was getting out of hand; it seemed as though nothing was beyond reach and anyone could get credit in one form or another. People were collecting credit cards like we used to collect cigarette cards back in the 1950s, in bundles. We stuffed them into special credit card wallets that had lots of individual pouches to hold them all – and of course we paid for these special wallets using one of our credit cards. In every retail park around the country you would see carpet and furniture stores offering interest-free credit with nothing to pay for the first year and then payments spread over three or four years. The furnishings would wear out before they were paid for. Sales staff accosted us in large department stores offering us special discounts if we filled in an application form for one of their own-brand credit cards there and then. It seemed impossible for us to avoid credit. It was being rammed down our throats all of the time. This was difficult for most strong-minded people to deal with but almost impossible for the weak, especially the hard up and vulnerable. From the latest mobile phones to holiday homes in the sun, we wanted as many luxury items as we could get to make our lifestyles better and better. However, to maintain this high standard of living we needed a regular source of income and so it was more important than ever for us to keep our jobs, and even find ways to earn more money doing second jobs, working longer hours or gaining promotion. The desire to have nice homes, motorcars and holidays was greater than it had ever been, as was the pressure to finance them.

At work, the culture of working long hours began in the 1980s but it picked up a pace in the 1990s as we became even more fearful of any fall in income. Many of us turned into workaholics, not necessarily because of an insurmountable workload but often just to be seen as hardworking and thereby protect our jobs. The traditional 9–5 culture in office jobs was disappearing, as were lunch breaks and being home for tea at 6.00 p.m. Often, although office workers and managers were being paid to work a 9–5 day, they were in fact working much longer hours at the office and many were even taking work home. This relatively new form of work ethic was infectious and it was becoming the norm for workers to work longer hours for no extra money. It was turning into a contest between work colleagues as to who could stay latest in the office and who could get there first in the morning. By the late 1990s, a quarter of workers in Britain were working more than forty-five hours a week. Employers revelled in the benefits of this new culture and many now expected office workers to take on extra workloads and work longer hours without being paid for it. Companies began building this extra resource into their calculations when assessing staffing levels. Office workers didn't realise it but they were actually adding to the risk of losing their jobs through redundancy because employers could now make do with fewer staff members. This created an unhealthily competitive atmosphere in offices with everyone trying to impress the boss with their willingness to work harder and for longer, even giving up holiday time to put in more hours and meet deadlines. This new culture meant that people were now living to work rather than working to live. The 1990s lifestyle we craved came at a tremendous cost to anyone caught up in this workaholic madness, and the trend was gaining in pace. There seemed to be no way of stopping it. If you were fortunate enough to have a good and well-paid job then you had to work hard to hold onto it. These days of must-have goods and easy credit facilities significantly increased the number of bills we had to pay each month and few of us were debt free. Families were often reliant upon the income from two wage earners, and women with young children were finding it hard to fit into the culture of working long hours; somehow, they had to find ways to maintain a reasonable standard of family life while managing the increasing demands of their working life. The more senior their job, the harder it was and they became increasingly reliant on others to care for their children while they put in the extra hours at work.

The culture of hard work and long hours meant that employers could keep staffing levels lean, but this only worked if everyone was suitably qualified and they all pulled their weight. Consequently, employers were becoming more discerning in their choice of employees. By now, in the main, it was our generation of baby boomers who were the employers and we were not finding it easy to track down suitable job applicants, especially when looking for young employees. Despite the supposed increasing standards of education it was surprisingly difficult to find suitably well-educated young people to fill jobs. In the early 1960s, the number of students in higher education hovered around 200,000, about 5% of the UK school population. By the mid-1990s, 1.6 million young people were in higher education; about 14% of the UK school population, and the numbers were heading upwards. Doubts were being raised as to how so many students could be clever enough to get into higher education. Had teaching standards really improved that much? Were young people brighter than they used to be? In 1992, John Major's Conservative government had made it possible for the old-style polytechnics to become new universities and so almost overnight, students who were previously not good enough to get into a university found themselves attending one of the new ex-polytechnic universities. People were also questioning whether the authorities were dumbing down modern-day examinations to ease the way for more students to enter university, keeping them off the dole and out of the unemployment figures. It was puzzling how so many graduates could leave university with a degree, expecting to get a good job, when they lacked the basic skills of spelling and simple arithmetic; many were unable to compose a letter because they had such a poor grasp of English grammar and some were only able to speak in a series of grunts. Increasing numbers of employers were distrusting modern-day qualifications and setting their own tests for job applicants.

It was in the 1990s, as 40-somethings, that many of us began to show the first signs of aging, and it wasn't just that policemen were looking younger as we got older. We pioneers of the so-called 1960s 'permissive society' were quietly maturing and most of us accepted the fact that we were no longer the social revolutionaries we once were. Whole new generations had grown up behind us and the world had moved on. Social attitudes had changed a lot in twenty-five years and we, the once carefree rebels of the 1960s, were finding ourselves shocked at how much youth rebelliousness, drug use and sexual freedom had escalated over the years. We began to moan about bad manners and lack of respect, and we despaired at the amount of graffiti we saw daubed on buildings everywhere we went. It was becoming unfashionable to say 'please' and 'thank you' or to hold the door open for someone else to pass through; people stopped forming queues at bus stops and the common courtesy of giving up one's seat for an old person or a pregnant women seemed to be abandoned altogether. The media blamed the liberal 1960s generation for the collapse in traditional values and perhaps they were right; after all, it was our generation that let the genie out of the bottle and broken all of the time-honoured rules. However, as 1960s teenagers, for as much as we sought to break with conventionality, we did maintain a reasonable standard of good manners and although we thought that anyone over the age of 40 was 'past it' and close to 'knocking on heaven's door', we did have respect for our elders and there was certainly no evidence of old people being mugged in the street. Since the 1960s, there has been a noticeable decline in standards of behaviour and as we moved through the 1990s there was no sign that things were getting any better.

A few years had now passed since we first began to admit that our fitness levels were not what they used to be, and despite the promising advertising slogan, 'Philosan fortifies the over forties,' we found that health supplements didn't actually roll back the years. The picture we saw in the mirror each morning wasn't quite as perfect as it had once been – lo and behold, another decade had gone by and many of us baby boomers were creeping ever closer to the big 5-O landmark. Yes, we would soon be 50-somethings and not quite as fabulous anymore. We were already developing some of the typical tell-tale signs of aging. Products like Sanatogen and Steradent now infiltrated our bathroom cabinets. We were becoming more aware of our health and some of us were even monitoring our own blood pressures and heart rates. We no longer burned off the calories as easily as we used to and so we began to watch our weight more carefully, avoiding fatty foods that were loaded with cholesterol. We moaned about the quality of modern-day newspaper print, refusing to accept the fact that our eyesight was failing and we needed to purchase some reading glasses. The smokers among us took to chewing gum as they desperately tried to kick the smoking habit and some were using the recently invented nicotine patches that promised to help overcome the craving to smoke. In the 1970s and 1980s it had become acceptable for young men to wear make-up and to colour their hair in the name of fashion, but in the 1990s those once young men were finding their natural hair colour turning to grey and they were now colouring their hair to preserve their youthful looks. The fashionable tints of the past were no longer of interest to aging baby boomer men. They were now using more functional male hair-colouring products like Grecian 2000. Meanwhile, the women were dieting like mad and heading back to the gym in a desperate attempt to regain their trim 1960s figures. We may by then have been starting to show signs of aging but we had one thing going for us and that was the fact that we were the most youthful generation of 40-somethings there had ever been and we were determined not to turn into replicas of our grandparents. We were once the ultramodern generation of the 1960s and although more than two decades had passed since then, most of us still felt young at heart. We might have been fast-approaching 50 and a bit knackered but we weren't ready to give up wearing the t-shirts and jeans of our youth. The clues of our middle age were all around us but still we refused to accept the label. By now, some of us had grandchildren of our own but that didn't mean we had to take on the appearance of being old fogies. We had no intention of growing old gracefully as our grandparents had done – there would be no grey cardigans and slippers for us. Okay, so we were no longer going out to all-night raves in draughty warehouses and head banging to the sounds of drum'n'bass. Yes, we did by now prefer to be locked inside our cosy homes rediscovering the simple joy of Ovaltine at bedtime. That didn't mean we were getting old – we were just maturing nicely, accepting the fact that for us discothèques were a thing of the past and that night-time was a time for sleeping.

seven

Into the Twenty-first Century

Older and Wiser

The New Year Millennium celebrations, headlined by events at the newly constructed Millennium Dome in Greenwich, South East London, were bigger and better than we had ever before seen. Speaking about the celebrations at the time, Prime Minister Tony Blair said that he observed a 'real sense of confidence and optimism'. 'You just wanted to bottle it and keep it,' he said. London's Thames-side festival of fireworks, light and music certainly inspired our optimism. We were entering the twenty-first century, turning a new page, and we were all hopeful of better times ahead.

As clocks struck noon on New Year's Day 2000, church bells began to peal all over the country as more than 2,000 churches rang in the third millennium. Little did we know that those church bells were in fact heralding in an era that would forever be remembered as the time of the world's worst ever terrorist mass-murders. The early years of the twenty-first century would also bear witness to the worst ever financial crisis the world had ever know, one that would lead to the British government having to fund a £550 billion banking rescue package in loans and guarantees to help stabilise the British banking system.

The first decade of the twenty-first century was given the name 'noughties'. Once again, we found ourselves in a period that was packed with a series of life-changing events; there were many good things happening as well as some downright awful ones. Unemployment was hovering around the 1.5 million mark for the first half of the decade but then it began to rise and by the end of 2009 the number had risen to just under 2.5 million, the highest figure for fifteen years. The numbers fell back slightly in 2010 but then began to rise again and by the end of 2011 there were 2.67 million people unemployed in the UK, 8.4% of the workforce – a seventeen-year high. We also suffered with health problems, in both humans and animals; there was the ongoing issue with mad cow disease (BSE) and by August 2000 the British pig industry was in crisis with an outbreak of swine fever. In February 2001, we were hit with a foot-and-mouth crisis, which resulted in 10 million sheep and cattle being killed, and in 2009 we humans suffered an outbreak of swine flu (H1N1 influenza).

We had grown used to public unrest in Britain and we had plenty of that during the early years of the twenty-first century. We had all sorts of protesters on our streets, some peaceful but many violent; from the high fuel price protesters to the anti-capitalist protesters, government budget cut protesters to students demonstrating against student fees – we had them all. Sometimes it was hard to establish the core subject of a protest because the banners often carried a choice of messages and slogans. We also had to put up with general rioting, looting and arson, as was the case with the August 2011 riots that took place in several London boroughs and other towns and cities across England. The scenes of rioting were horrific, with burning buildings, frenzied looting and hundreds of thugs running amok. At least five deaths were reported as being linked to this outbreak of rioting and there were 206 people listed as injured, mostly police officers (186). Five police dogs also suffered injuries and there was an estimated £200 million worth of property damage. There were a number of other outbreaks of disorder and also some race riots from 2000 to 2012, mostly in the London area, West Midlands and the North of England. The level of violent disorder we saw on our streets during that period was awful but the acts of terrorism we witnessed during the early 2000s were shocking beyond words.

The world as we knew it changed forever on 11 September 2001 when nineteen al-Qaeda terrorists hijacked four passenger planes over the United States and used them as weapons in their suicide mission of mass-killings and destruction. We watched replay after replay of these horrific events on television for days and weeks afterwards, and it was still hard to accept the reality of what had happened. We asked ourselves over and over again, how could anyone, let alone a whole group of people, be so wicked? It was like watching computer-generated images; we had never before witnessed such graphic scenes of wilful killing and destruction. The hijackers intentionally crashed two of the passenger planes into the landmark Twin Towers of the World Trade Center in New York City, and another into the Pentagon in Arlington, Virginia. The fourth passenger plane was targeting Washington but it crashed into a field near Shanksville in Pennsylvania after passengers tried to overcome the hijackers. In all, 2,977 innocent victims were killed, including all of the 246 plane passengers. The nineteen hijackers also died. These shocking events have come to be known as the September 11 attacks, and often referred to as 9/11. By now, here in the UK we were well used to high levels of security because of the frequent IRA terrorist attacks, but the CCTV security cameras that littered all of our main streets and in particular those that had been used to form a 6.5-mile ring of steel around the City of London since 1993, were all put there to protect us against car bombers. We were used to dealing with terrorists who would leave explosive devices in public places and then make their escape, people who wanted to get away without being identified. We were now dealing with a whole new security problem: fanatical suicide killers who didn't care if they were identified. Following the September 11 attacks, security measures were strengthened around the world and none more so than here in the UK. It now seemed as though everywhere we went, whether out on the street or inside buildings, CCTV cameras monitored us. If we drove into the City of London our vehicle registration plates were automatically photographed, traced and tracked, and the police were even stopping people from taking photographs that might capture the image of a public building, even if only in the background. Our bags were routinely being searched when we entered public buildings and even business premises. We became very aware that ordinary, innocent people were now much more vulnerable to terrorist attacks than ever before. We became very suspicious of people, especially anyone carrying a holdall or something suitable to transport an explosive device. There was a great feeling of insecurity, especially in the towns and cities. Sadly, our worst fears were realised on 7 July 2005 (7/7) when there was a series of co-ordinated terrorist bombings on London's public transport system during the morning rush hour. The terrorists had planned for all four bombs they were carrying to explode at exactly the same time. Three exploded within the same minute on three London Underground trains, and the fourth exploded one hour later on a double-decker bus in Tavistock Square, London. Fifty-two innocent people were killed and more than 700 were injured in the attacks; the bombers also died. What made the attacks even more shocking was that the killers were home-grown Islamic terrorists who were all living in England at the time of the attacks, all harbouring extreme views and beliefs and willing to carry out indiscriminate mass-killings. Their victims were innocent civilians travelling on public transport; most were just on their way to work.

Two weeks later, at around midday on 21 July, there were a further four attempted bomb attacks in London, at Shepherd's Bush, Warren Street and Oval stations on London's Underground, and on a bus in Shoreditch. A fifth homemade bomb was later found in bushes in West London and it was suspected that there had been a fifth bomber who had dumped it there and fled. Fortunately, nobody was killed or injured because only the detonators of the bombs exploded and not the bombs that had been intended to kill a large number of innocent people.

If all of this killing, maiming and destruction wasn't enough for us to endure, our country was involved in on-going conflicts overseas and we regularly witnessed scenes of soldiers arriving home in flag-draped coffins. There was the war in Afghanistan (2001 onwards), the Iraq War (2003–2009) and what is now called the Libyan Intervention (2011). So far, the early years of the twenty-first century have been filled with terrorism, war and general unrest. However, there was at least some good and long-awaited news on terrorism in July 2005, when we heard that the IRA had ordered an end to its armed campaign and two months later General John de Chastelain, head of the Independent International Commission on Decommissioning that was set up as part of the Northern Ireland peace process, announced that the Provisional IRA had put their arsenal of weapons 'beyond use'. That didn't signal a complete end to Northern Ireland-related troubles because there were different factions of the IRA and also loyalist paramilitary groups that disagreed with the terms of the peace agreements, but it did bring to an end to most of the violence.

With all of these sorry events going on in our lives, you would think that we had little time to worry about anything else, but since 2007 our lives have in fact been dominated by the Global Financial Crisis and, more importantly, the UK financial crisis, which has greatly affected all of our lives, still is, and will do for years to come. This financial crisis took us into a prolonged period of austerity and it almost bankrupted our country. It stirred up tremendous resentment among the British public who saw the government's bank rescue package as simply a bailout for rich bankers. It seemed as though innocent, hardworking, tax-paying people were bailing out rich bankers while at the same time paying the cost of the bailout in cutbacks and job losses. Some of the blameless casualties of the financial crisis would never be able to find work again. It was a terrible state of affairs and it would take years to solve. Just to crown all of the serious issues of the early years of the twenty-first century, here in Britain we actually had a couple of earthquakes, big enough to be felt across most of the country. The first of these was in Dudley in 2002, and the other one was in Lincolnshire in 2008. Each and every year we think that we get a lot of rain in the UK but in 2009 we got an awful lot in one day; well at least one place did – Seathwaite in the Lake District in Cumbria had a total rainfall of 314.4 mm in twenty-four hours, which is a UK record for the amount of rainfall in a single location in any twenty-four-hour period. Mind you,

Seathwaite is considered to be the wettest inhabited place in England.

In each passing decade, we baby boomers have witnessed much change, mostly to our benefit but some less so. We look back fondly on things that have completely disappeared from our lives and we question some of the changing rules and regulations that have influenced the way we live our lives. In the early years of the twenty-first century we have seen and lost even more things from our past – some we miss greatly and others not at all – but they all stir up memories of bygone days; each event is part of a chapter in our lives. In 2000, the old Wembley Stadium closed down and the bulldozers moved in to demolish the famous twin towers that had stood proudly for seventy-seven years as millions of football supporters passed beneath. To add to our woes, in the last ever game to be played at the old Wembley Stadium, the England football team lost 1–0 to Germany and the England manager, Kevin Keegan, resigned after the game. Three weeks later, on 30 October 2000, the Football Association appointed the England team's first ever foreign manager, the Swedish coach Sven-Goran Eriksson. In 2002, Queen Elizabeth, the Queen Mother, died at the age of 101. Her daughter, Princess Margaret, the Queen's younger sister, also died that year at the age of 71. We had watched news coverage of them both throughout our entire lives and we knew a lot about them; they seemed so much a part of our lives right from childhood and now they were gone. In 2003, after gracing our skies for twenty-seven years with its stunning streamline looks, Concorde, the supersonic aircraft, made its final commercial flight. In that same year, we saw Britain's first toll motorway open when the M6 Toll came into service in the West Midlands. And, who would have thought that old hell raiser Mick Jagger of Rolling Stones fame would ever be offered, accept and receive a knighthood for his services to music, and to be knighted by the Prince of Wales, Prince Charles, who is himself a vintage 1948 post-war baby boomer?

In 2004, the Football League of England and Wales was rebranded, causing great confusion to all but the most educated football fans. The old Division One became the Football League Championship, the old Division Two became League One, and the old Division Three became League Two. It seemed as though every team had suddenly moved up a league, but it was in name only. The following year, in November 2005, the football world said goodbye to George Best who died at the age of 59. Everyone knew who George Best was: an iconic sporting and playboy figure of the 1960s and 1970s; probably the first football superstar; always in the headlines. A couple of years down the line, in 2007, we saw the final edition of BBC's *Grandstand* sports programme. It had been on our television screens and in our lives for forty-nine years when it ended. In that same year, the Labour Party politician Jacqui Smith made history when she became the first ever female home secretary. She made headlines again in 2009 when she stood down as home secretary following an investigation into the MPs' expenses scandal when she was found to have broken the rules on second-home expenses.

She subsequently lost her seat as Member of Parliament for Redditch. The misuse of expenses by MPs became a huge political scandal fuelled by information leaked to the Telegraph Group of newspapers; many MPs were found to be at fault, some apologised and/or resigned while others faced criminal charges and a few even went to prison. In 2009, we also saw the 35-year-old ITV Teletext service discontinued, and in 2011 we found we could no longer use our cheque guarantee cards; some shops and garages even stopped accepting cheques as a form of payment – a massive milestone. And, in July that year we waved goodbye to the *News of the World* newspaper following a phone-hacking scandal. The final edition, after having been in circulation for 168 years, was on Sunday 10 July 2011. On 26 February 2012, the first edition of *The Sun on Sunday* newspaper went on sale, replacing the defunct *News of the World* (both owned by the NI Group). We had long since grown used to seeing long-established shop names disappearing from the high streets and shopping malls and now we had even more names to add to our list: Littlewoods stores disappeared in 2005 after sixty-eight years on our high streets, many of them converted into Primark stores; and then there were the Woolworths stores that for so long were the mainstay of our high streets; we all shopped in our local Woolworths store and we came to rely on them for all sorts of bits and pieces. They were all closed down over Christmas 2008/09 when the firm went out of business. We all probably knew someone who worked in a Woolworths store at some time or another – 27,450 jobs were lost when they ceased trading. MFI also went out of business in 2008; many of us still have their furniture in our homes – all of that self-assembled occasional furniture and the white and magnolia bedroom suites. In 2005, for the first time, pubs in England and Wales were permitted to open for twenty-four hours, and in 2007 a ban was imposed on smoking in public places (2006 in Scotland). In 2005 we all got issued with new 'chip and pin' smart credit, debit and ATM cards, so we no longer had to sign credit card slips. In 2005, we saw the first gay weddings when civil partnerships became legal. And, that same year, more ground-breaking history was made when fox hunting and other types of hunting with dogs was made unlawful in England and Wales (2002 in Scotland). However, the most important and welcome change in recent years, as far as anyone who is fast approaching retirement age is concerned, relates to age and it directly affects all post-war baby boomers; there is now no longer a mandatory retirement age in the UK and employers cannot force workers to leave when they reach 65 unless it can be objectively justified. And, for the first time, age is now part of the UK equal rights rules. Employers must now give equal treatment in access to employment as well as private and public services regardless of someone's age. We could have done with that rule when we were 45 and we were already considered to be over the hill.

The 2010s kicked off with a high level of celebration; first there was the royal wedding of Prince William and Kate Middleton on 29 April 2011, which was marked by a public holiday. Then the Queen's Diamond Jubilee celebrations, which were centred around the first weekend in

June 2012 and marked with an additional public holiday tagged onto the spring bank holiday. Bradley Wiggins won the Tour de France and we enjoyed worldwide acclaim when we hosted the prestigious London 2012 Summer Olympics. The last time London hosted the Olympics was in 1948, right in the middle of the post-war baby boom period.

In July 2000, after thirty-two years, the Ford Motor Company ended production of the Ford Escort car. It was one of the top three bestselling cars in Britain for much of that time and was especially popular in the 1980s when it commanded the top position from 1982–89, only missing out to the Ford Cortina for the top spot in 1980–81. It had recently been displaced by new the Ford Fiesta and Ford Focus cars. The Ford Focus was by now well entrenched as the bestselling car in Britain each year and it remained so until the Ford Fiesta took over the mantle in 2009. Most of us never shed a tear at the demise of the Ford Escort in 2000, but I am sure that the majority of us felt a twinge of sadness when production of the iconic Mini ended that same year. The Mini had been part of our lives for forty-one years and it was our dream car when we first started work back in the 1960s. However, production was to start the following year on a newly designed model and the good news was that we might not need to spend as much time under the bonnet of the new Mini because this version was to be made by BMW and it would be called the BMW Mini One. We also shed a tear in 2005 when the last British-owned volume car maker, MG Rover, went into administration and the iconic eighty-year-old

British-made MG brand was transferred to a company in China. The one piece of good news for car enthusiasts is that Range Rover is still going strong after forty-two years (est. 1970) and in 2010 the 1 millionth Range Rover came off the production line.

We have enjoyed the benefits of evolution, and we have seen massive improvements in lifestyles but along the way we seem to have given up so much of what was good about the traditional British way of life. Since the Second World War, successive governments have imposed all sorts of new rules and regulations upon us under the guises of necessary progress, world peace, trade, security and defence. They have gradually dismantled our country's sovereignty and handed over many of the important decision-making responsibilities to an unelected body of overseas-based bureaucrats. To make matters worse, they have committed us to paying huge annual membership fees for the privilege of belonging to this non-exclusive, failing and dysfunctional European club that is run by hordes of political fat cats who seem to grow richer by the day. We seem to have lost control of our country and we have even lost control of who can come and live here, and how we live our lives. Successive post-war governments have overseen the gradual demise of our country's unique identity that was once recognised the world over. In recent years, our borders have been left ajar to allow all and sundry to come in. Britain has been transformed into an overpopulated and disjointed multicultural nation. Our government no longer knows what the true population of our country is. Many of our politicians relish in the fact that they have been instrumental in changing Britain into a multicultural nation, but we now have a population with a confused mixture of allegiances, and we no longer have a common first language. Our politicians have changed the cultural identity of our nation without asking the indigenous population if they wanted such a fundamental and irreversible change to take place.

At work, the idea of jobs for life disappeared into the mist during the 1970s and 1980s, and it is now generally accepted that there is no longer any such thing as job security. Gone are the days of working for one employer for the whole of your working life. The likelihood is that you will now, at best, have several different jobs and employers in the course of your lifetime, and at worst, you will be out of work for long periods at a time. However, changes to employment laws over the years have given workers more entitlements and rights than ever before. Unlike in the 1970s, workers no longer need unions so much to fight their corner. Employers now have all sorts of record keeping, form filling, procedures and rules to follow before they can sack someone, and employees now have the means to dispute any actions their employers might take to alter their job. Government-imposed red tape makes it very difficult for an employer to get rid of a bad worker and more and more workers are taking legal advice regarding employment issues, and taking action against their employers. By the mid-2000s, the number of employment tribunal cases being heard was more than double the amount there was in the mid-1990s. By 2010, the number had increased further still; there were about 230,000 compared to 90,000 in 1995.

The kind of work we do has also been changing with each passing decade and as we move through the 2010s, if you have a job then it is very likely that you work in retailing or in finance or in one of the business-service sectors. Forty years ago one-third of us worked in manufacturing, whereas today it's only one in five, and reducing all the time. Today, if you work in a large, open-plan office then the chances are you work in one of the thousands of call centres that have been created since the 1970s. These are the factories of the twenty-first century but the only things they make are telephone calls. In recent years, even call centre jobs have become insecure as big employers found ways of reducing costs, often by moving call centre jobs to countries offering cheap, well-educated labour, such as India. Each year increasing numbers of us work from home, often hot-desking (sharing one desk) when we need to be at the office. The improving efficiency of communication technology now makes this so easy; with email and the Internet, smart phones and web-cams, we can work anywhere just as long as we have access to broadband. The down side of this is that we are now never off duty; we are contactable twenty-four hours a day and we can be expected to do even more work from home than ever before. It is now very difficult to separate work from our home life. The experience of travelling to a workplace is so different to how it used to be; few people read newspapers on public transport, everyone is either doing something on their smart phones and iPads or reading ebooks on ereaders, such as the Kindle or Kobo; nobody carries a briefcase anymore, it's all laptop cases, wheeled flight-bags and backpacks. When we get to work, everyone now talks in a strange jargon that has been developing since the 1990s. Anyone returning to work after years away from it and expecting to find clipboards and flipcharts are in for a shock; they will need a jargon translator. For example, this 'desk-jockey' needs to find 'solutions' to the 'elephant in the room'. It's a 'big ask' but not 'rocket science'. Afterwards we'll do some 'blamestorming'. For the uninitiated, what this jargon actually means is: this desk-bound office worker who is dealing with lots of phone calls, text messages and emails all at once and dare not leave his/her desk needs to find answers to a big problem that is obvious to all but everyone is trying to ignore. It's a lot to expect from him/her but it's not that difficult. After he/she has dealt with it we will have a meeting to establish whose fault it was ... simple! We won't delve into any of the other mysteries of today's workplace jargon and practices, like 'lean manufacturing', 'key performance indicators', 'mission statements', and 'team-building away-days'. Goodness knows what they are about.

People wonder why we post-war baby boomers look back on the 1950s and 1960s with such affection when we enjoy such rich lives today. It's not that we long to return to the austere lifestyle of the 1950s and the youthful heady days of the 1960s. We don't miss living in cold and damp conditions and having to go without things. It's more the camaraderie of people and the way of life that we remember with such great fondness. Yes, we were young and we saw life through young eyes, but life was much more relaxed, friendly and peaceful than it is today. We remember the quiet and traffic-free streets of the 1950s, and the busy high streets full of friendly shopkeepers, proper bus queues with people standing in line and bus conductors who waited for you when you were rushing for a bus. Those were the days when fast food meant a doorstep of bread and butter, and central heating meant a warm glow from an open fire. We lived among neighbours rather than in communities and we didn't need such things as community leaders because everyone pulled together in times of crisis. Britain had a national identity that was recognised the world over; we knew and trusted our neighbours and felt we had a common purpose in life; we felt safe and unthreatened; we didn't know what terrorism was; we lived much simpler lives and children retained their innocence through to their teenage years. There was a lot of humility, pride and dignity, and people were very trusting and tended to take other people at face value, and in austere times people were generous with what they had.

When we were children in the 1950s, we saw patched-up ex-soldiers on crutches, forced to scrape a living selling boxes of matches from a tray on street corners. It was a time when the word poor really meant poor – potless, starving, clothed in rags – and there was much evidence of this in all of our towns and cities, particularly in run-down and slum areas. In Britain today, poverty has taken on a whole new meaning.

We now live in a materialistic throw-away society in which there are people who consider themselves poor if they can't afford the latest widescreen television. In the 1950s, a classy pair of shoes was a pair without holes in them. Many a child passed their 11-plus exams but never went to grammar school because their parents couldn't afford to buy the school uniform. There were no cheap school uniform deals from the likes of Tesco and Asda back then; you had to buy the complete outfit from one of the designated school uniform shops and everything was expensive, as were the leather satchels and bags for your school books, not to mention the gym-kits, football boots, hockey sticks and all the other paraphernalia. The best you could do as far as a bargain was concerned was to buy your shirts, blouses and socks from your local Woolworths on the high street. You also had to be able to afford travelling costs because grammar schools were few and far between. Some people did two or three jobs just so they could earn enough to pay the rent on nothing more than a slum property, often owned by an unscrupulous Rachman-type landlord. We don't want to go back to those days of hardship but along the way something has gone wrong with the way Britain's welfare system has evolved.

I loved the whole atmosphere of the 1950s country I grew up in. I could have done without all of those brutal and overzealous canings I got at school, but it was the fear of those beatings that kept us young chancers in check. Times were hard but as youngsters we knew no better and we just got on with life. The nearest thing we had to a mobile phone was two tin cans joined together by a long piece of string and then stretched across the road and pulled tightly. We shouted into those tin cans and we thought that we could hear what each other was saying from several yards apart, but we were just kidding ourselves; we were usually shouting so loudly into the tin cans that everyone in the next street could hear us. It is incredible how far things have advanced since we were children in the 1950s. Kids don't use old tin cans to communicate with each other anymore; they now use mobile phones, iPads and computers to keep in touch with one another through the Internet. They have hundreds of what they call 'virtual friends' whom they meet over the Internet using social networking websites such as Facebook, Twitter, Linkedin and MySpace. Many have never met each other face to face and they don't actually know all of their virtual friends personally. They just consider themselves to be like-minded with the same kind of interests and they use the social networking websites to link up with each other to chat and exchange information. Having never met doesn't seem to matter when it comes to disclosing personal information and photographs. It's a very strange cyber-world that many of us baby boomers find hard to understand. It's a sort of modern-day version of pen pals, except you don't have to pay for postage and wait for a reply, and with this modern version you can have hundreds of pen pals all sharing the same information at the same time. If you want to be really sharing you can open a Twitter account and you can leave short messages for the whole world to see. You can tweet

about everything and nothing, and you can tell everyone what you are doing and where you are going for every minute of the day. All of this is posted on the Internet for all to see, but who really cares? Well, it seems that the 900 million worldwide registered users of Facebook care, and so do the 500 million worldwide Twitter users. About 46% of Facebook users are aged 13–25, which is not surprising, but 5% of Facebook users are in the 55–65 age group and that number is growing. I would imagine that most of the older users of Facebook only use it to communicate with known friends and family. Any of us who do use it to communicate with virtual friends probably need to get out more. In this modern age, friends and family are often spread far and wide apart and the Internet makes it easy to communicate instantly with them to exchange information and pictures, and even talk to them and do one-to-one video calling for free.

No child will ever again experience the joys of a 1950s childhood with all of the freedom and innocence we once knew. In the 1960s, we had the best teenage years you could ever wish for and we will go on to become the most youthful older generation there has ever been. We have certainly come a very long way since the days of shouting into tin cans and playing hopscotch on the pavements. There has been a whole lifetime of change and we have adapted to it well and embraced much of it, but we post-war baby boomers will never forget how it all started for us: the tin baths, outside lavatories and doorsteps of bread and dripping. Our 1960s slogan, 'Turn on, Tune in and Drop out,' has now for us become, 'Turn on, Tune

in and Drop off.' Who would ever have thought our journey through life would be so eventful? We have seen and done it all and along the way we bought most of the T-shirts. We are lucky to have so many memories to reflect upon.